S. Hrg. 114–81

ADDRESSING THE NEED FOR VICTIM SERVICES IN INDIAN COUNTRY

HEARING

BEFORE THE

COMMITTEE ON INDIAN AFFAIRS
UNITED STATES SENATE

ONE HUNDRED FOURTEENTH CONGRESS

FIRST SESSION

JUNE 10, 2015

Printed for the use of the Committee on Indian Affairs

U.S. GOVERNMENT PUBLISHING OFFICE

96–925 PDF   WASHINGTON : 2015

For sale by the Superintendent of Documents, U.S. Government Publishing Office
Internet: bookstore.gpo.gov   Phone: toll free (866) 512–1800; DC area (202) 512–1800
Fax: (202) 512–2104   Mail: Stop IDCC, Washington, DC 20402–0001

CONTENTS

ADDRESSING THE NEED FOR VICTIM SERVICES IN INDIAN COUNTRY

WEDNESDAY, JUNE 10, 2015

U.S. SENATE,
COMMITTEE ON INDIAN AFFAIRS,
Washington, DC.

The Committee met, pursuant to notice, at 2:30 p.m. in room 628, Dirksen Senate Office Building, Hon. John Barrasso, Chairman of the Committee, presiding.

OPENING STATEMENT OF HON. JOHN BARRASSO, U.S. SENATOR FROM WYOMING

The CHAIRMAN. I would now like to call to order the meeting of the Indian Affairs Committee and ask the witnesses to please come forward.

Today the Committee's hearing is on Addressing the Need for Victim Services in Indian Country. This Committee has examined crime and justice in Indian communities for several years and I have made criminal justice a priority as chairman.

Federal data shows that Indian communities face some of the highest victimization rates in the Country. Native youth experience violent crime rates up to ten times the national rate. Violence is pervasive and tied to 75 percent of deaths among American Indian and Alaska Natives between the ages of 12 and 20.

American Indian women are murdered at a rate of more than ten times the national average on some reservations. It is clear that tribes lack the resources and capacity to provide basic services to victims of crime on their lands.

The primary source of victim assistance funding is the Crime Victims Fund. Unfortunately, the way this fund is currently administered, it is not working for Native victims of crime. Under the current system, only a portion of this money reaches the States, and far less ever reaches Indian Country. Instead of accessing victim assistance and compensation grants directly from the Crime Victims Fund like other States and territories, tribes must apply to the States for these resources.

Despite the exceedingly high crime rates and great need for victim services in Indian Country, over the last five years, tribes have never received more than 0.7 percent of the Crime Victims Fund available for victim assistance. We will hear today that one of the underlying problems is that most tribes lag far behind the rest of the Nation when it comes to baseline crime victim infrastructure and capacity.

(1)

For example, most tribe do not have emergency shelters for crime victims. Most tribes do not have facilities or personnel for the delivery of critical services, such as medical care and counseling. Most tribes cannot provide temporary or transitional housing, even when the perpetrators live in the same home as the victim. This gap must be addressed as it severely limits tribes' ability to deliver even the most basic crime victim services and in turn limits opportunities to restore safety and security to Native communities.

We must expand tribal access to resources for crime victim services, improve the way these Federal dollars are administered and ensure that tribes have the flexibility to develop programs that meet the needs of their respective communities.

So I look forward to hearing from our witnesses today on how to best accomplish these goals. I will be releasing a plan in the near future to change the status quo for Native victims of crime.

Before we hear from the witnesses present today, I want to recognize the Vice Chairman for an opening statement.

STATEMENT OF HON. JON TESTER,
U.S. SENATOR FROM MONTANA

Senator TESTER. Thank you, Chairman Barrasso. I appreciate your holding this important hearing on Addressing the Need for Victim Services in Indian Country.

Study after study shows that crime has devastating impacts on its victims. Often those effects are not the easiest topics to discuss.

For the witnesses who we have here today, I know that this is not a topic that any of you would like to dwell on either. Yet crime is a reality in far too many communities and far too many homes in Indian Country. Each of the witnesses here today have been touched by this issue in very personal ways. And each of you works very hard every day to help curb violence, be it suicide, domestic violence or drug or alcohol abuse.

I just want to say how much I appreciate the work that you do, and I appreciate your coming here today to share your knowledge and your experience with us. I would just like to say, we talk about issues a lot. Hopefully we can stop talking about this issue and start addressing it.

I want to extend a personal welcome to Chairman Rusty Stafne of the Fort Peck Assiniboine and Sioux Tribes in my home State of Montana. The Fort Peck Reservation is located in the northeast corner of our State and lies within the boundaries of one of the highest growing crime regions in the Country. Let me say that again: it lies within the boundaries of one of the highest growing crime regions in the Country. That region is known as the Bakken.

This past August, I held a listening session focusing on the human trafficking in the Bakken region. We have heard first-hand how this unprecedented economic opportunity has brought increased population, increased traffic and unfortunately, increased crime into this very rural part of our Country.

Chairman Stafne certainly knows better than most how all of this translates into an uptick in crime and violence in his community. Fort Peck has been a leader in addressing issues of violent crime on their reservation. As Chairman Stafne will discuss in his testimony, they were one of the first tribes in the Country to cross-deputize local, State and tribal law enforcement.

They also showed leadership in working directly with the National Native Children's Trauma Center out of the University of Montana in order to address the high instances of suicide and attempted suicide of Native youth in their community. Additionally, they were one of the first tribes to be selected as a pilot project site under the Violence Against Women Reauthorization Act of 2013.

Yet, there is much more to do. The tribe estimates that they have only 50 percent of the police force necessary to police their vast reservation. The resources that do exist are often fleeting and are anchored on temporary grant funding that prohibits stability or growth. I am certain this lack of consistent and dependable funding is a problem for all tribes, not just for those in Montana.

In recent years we have made some gains with the passage of the Tribal Law and Order Act, and more recently by strengthening tribal authority under the Violence Against Women Act. But we still need to do more in helping our tribal nations combat crime in their communities.

Our Committee will continue to work to secure resources from law enforcement and victim services in Indian Country. One such proposal I would like to thank our Chairman for working on would create a set-aside in funding, specifically for Indian Country out of the Crime Victims Fund created by the Victims of Crime Act. I think that this set-aside is an important step in creating safer communities in Indian Country. I will work with my colleagues to ensure this legislation represents the views of Indian Country, including those we are going to hear from here today.

Again, I want to thank everyone on the ground who works every day to improve the lives of our Native Americans and Native American children throughout Indian Country. I look forward to the testimony today.

Thank you, Mr. Chairman.

The CHAIRMAN. Thank you, Vice Chairman Tester.

Would any other members like to make an opening statement? Senator Crapo.

STATEMENT OF HON. MIKE CRAPO,
U.S. SENATOR FROM IDAHO

Senator CRAPO. Yes, Mr. Chairman, just briefly. Thank you for holding this important oversight hearing today. Among the critical issues facing Indian Country at the present time, criminal activity and victimization with tribal lands ranks as a top concern.

We are all aware of the influence of the Victims of Crime Act and the Violence Against Women Act, and I appreciate the efforts of the Chairman and Ranking Member to help us focus even more effectively on Indian land. It is the task of this Committee to ensure that Federal policies that are aimed at rectifying the problem are serving their intended purposes. We have all seen the data and know that Native American communities are disproportionately represented in crime and abuse when compared to the broader U.S. population. We must continue to seek ways in which they can be improved.

The Victims of Crime Act is one tool that Congress has adopted to help provide relief services and assistance. However, we know that a lack of parity presently exists regarding the share of the Crime Victims Fund going to tribal communities.

I look forward to hearing from today's witnesses and know that their feedback will help guide our efforts in addressing this discrepancy. Once again, Mr. Chairman, thank you for holding this hearing. I look forward to hearing from our witnesses.

The CHAIRMAN. Thank you, Senator Crapo.

Would anyone else like to make an opening statement? Senator Heitkamp.

STATEMENT OF HON. HEIDI HEITKAMP, U.S. SENATOR FROM NORTH DAKOTA

Senator HEITKAMP. Thank you, Mr. Chairman and Vice Chairman Tester for holding what I think is an absolutely critically important hearing today. As you know, North Dakota is home to five tribal reservations that are located almost exclusively in rural areas, which makes it really difficult to provide critical services.

I will tell you, I just was at a hearing where they talked about kids driving around Indian Country holding up a cell phone so that they could transmit electronically their papers to UND so they could be graded. Think about if that person was a victim of crime and they had no way to dial 911.

I can tell you, as a former attorney general, a huge gap in our collective services to protect people in my State comes as a result of a lack of official law enforcement on the reservations where they have major crime responsibilities. So this is an issue that we have all worked hard on, whether you are in Fort Peck or whether you are in Fort Berthold, as Senator Hoeven and I have experienced, these problems cross the reservation. We want them fixed, and we want victim services to be made available to all the victims of North Dakota, so that no one gets left behind.

So thank you so much for holding this hearing. We look forward to ongoing discussions about how we can improve victim services, but also law enforcement services in Indian Country and my State of North Dakota.

The CHAIRMAN. Thank you, Senator Heitkamp.

Any other members who wish to make an opening statement? If not, today we will be hearing from Director Darren Cruzan from the Office of Justice Services, Bureau of Indian Affairs. We will be hearing from, as introduced by Senator Tester, Chairman Rusty Stafne. Also Judge Dianne Barker Harrold from the Pawnee Nation of Oklahoma and Mr. Gerad Godfrey, who is the Chair of the Violent Crimes Compensation, Office of the Governor, from the State of Alaska.

Welcome, all of you. I want to remind each of the witnesses that your full written testimony will be made a part of the official hearing record. So please keep your statements to five minutes, so that we may have time for questions.

I look forward to hearing your testimony, beginning with Director Cruzan.

STATEMENT OF DARREN CRUZAN, DIRECTOR, OFFICE OF JUSTICE SERVICES, BUREAU OF INDIAN AFFAIRS, U.S. DEPARTMENT OF THE INTERIOR

Mr. CRUZAN. Chairman Barrasso, Vice Chairman Tester and the rest of the Committee, I want to thank you for allowing me to come and testify on this as has been said, very important issue.

I think crime in Indian Country, as you have all mentioned, is well documented. I don't need to convince you, you know that as well as I do, if not better.

I think that the exciting part of this conversation is what we could possibly do for these crime victims. Similar to what we did with our high priority performance initiative, but I think it is important for us to have the discussion and the understanding that the crimes that we are seeing in Indian Country are heinous.

And when we did our high priority performance initiative, we saw, because of the added resources that were put out there, a greater than 50 percent increase in violent crime in the first 12 months. That was not because more violent crime was being committed, it was because the community members saw that something was being done, there was more violent crime being reported.

I believe that we would see a similar increase in the number of violent crimes. There are virtually, I say virtually, for the vast majority of Indian Country, there are not the resources out there that are needed. These victims and their families, the survivors, are suffering because of it.

And it is a very simple thing, from initial response where there is emergency housing needed or there is transportation to get a rape kit done, all the way to the judicial process where hopefully ultimately the suspects in these violent offenses would be held accountable for their actions.

Far too many times in Indian Country, what we have are these victims that don't show up to court because they don't understand the system, they don't even have a way to get to these types of hearings.

So this is absolutely, as Senator Heitkamp said, an absolutely critically important conversation to be having. Just to give you a little bit of perspective of the Bureau of Indian Affairs and how we operate currently with our victims program, we, through a partnership with DOJ and specifically Office of Victims of Crime, we are able to receive funding, sort of similarly to how our tribal partners do, as seed money to initially hire these victim specialists who are the touch point for the victims and respond to the crime scenes and provide services.

We currently have ten for the BIA that serve in many locations. That is the total number that we have that are actually out there providing the services specifically to the BIA.

In 2014, these ten victim specialists had a combined total of 2,100 victims that they provided services to. That is a staggering number when you think of it as a whole number. But if you think about everything that goes into providing those services, there was over 16,000 services provided.

So it is, as I said, the rides to the hospital, it is the emergency services provided and maybe diapers to the family, those types of services that are being provided. That is 210 cases a year that each one of these victim specialists are providing.

They are in remote locations. They may be servicing four or five or more tribes with hundreds of miles distance in between them, responding 24 hours a day. Very, very difficult thing to do.

I think it is the lack of adequate sustainable funds that is the biggest concern for us. I do believe that we could have a significant impact if the resources were out there, us and our tribal partners, in providing services. I absolutely agree with what I heard today. It is equity that we are looking for, it is the ability for these victims who are suffering greatly to receive the services and hopefully heal from it.

I know there is another hearing, and I have 37 seconds here, I know there is another hearing coming up regarding suicide. I think there is a direct correlation between victimization and services or lack of services being provided.

I am happy to be here with this panel and I look forward to the questions.

[The prepared statement of Mr. Cruzan follows:]

PREPARED STATEMENT OF DARREN CRUZAN, DIRECTOR, OFFICE OF JUSTICE SERVICES, BUREAU OF INDIAN AFFAIRS, U.S. DEPARTMENT OF THE INTERIOR

Good afternoon, Chairman Barrasso, Vice Chairman Tester, and members of the Committee. Thank you for the opportunity to provide a statement on behalf of the Department of the Interior, Bureau of Indian Affairs, on the topic of ''Addressing the Need for Victim Services in Indian Country. I would like to take a moment to congratulate the Committee and members of Congress on taking unprecedented action that increased the cap on the Crime Victims Fund, a catalyst to improve and expand the Nation's capacity to effectively respond to the needs of all crime victims.

We at the Bureau of Indian Affairs share the commitment to meet the needs of crime victims in American Indian and Alaska Native communities and we also aim to decrease barriers faced by AI/AN communities to access programs and services critical to meeting the needs of crime victims.

The Department also appreciates and would like to thank the Office for Victims of Crime (OVC) at Department of Justice for its continued support. Since 2010 OVC has provided approximately $2.9 million in seed money to support BIA Victim Specialist positions in New Mexico, Montana, Arizona, and South Dakota. In FY 2015, OVC will be providing BIA an additional $832,000 for training and technical assistance including efforts focused on Pine Ridge and the Bakken region.

State of Indian Country

AI/AN communities make up approximately 1.7 percent of the Nation's population, but suffer some of the highest rates of violent crime, shorter life expectancy, higher rates of suicide, and have the least amount of consistent resources available on a continuum of care that one can expect in most rural and urban settings.

While there is a severe lack of data on crime and victimization in AI/AN communities, it is well documented that AI/AN communities experience higher rates of violence than the general population.

AI/AN women experience the highest rates of sexual assault and domestic violence in the nation. [1] Native youth between the ages of 12 and 19 are more likely than non-Native youth to be the victim of either serious violent crime or simple assault; [2] and suicide is the second leading cause of death for our Native youth aged 15 to 24. [3] Just in the last ninety (90) days, BIA Law Enforcement alone responded to eighty-eight (88) suicide attempts, with six (6) of those being successful attempts, accounting for almost one (1) suicide attempt per day. AI/AN children suffer post-

---

[1] www.BJS.gov.

[2] Indian Law and Order Commission Report, Chapter 6 *Juvenile Justice: Failing the Next Generation*, November 2013.

[3] Substance Abuse and Mental Health Services Administration (SAMHSA), National Survey on Drug Use and Health, 2003.

traumatic stress disorder at the same rate as veterans returning from Iraq and Afghanistan, and triple the rate of the general population. [4]

Forty percent of the federally-recognized tribes in the United States are in Alaska. Alaska Natives represent one-fifth of the total State population. [5] The demographics for Alaska Native villages are vastly different than most American Indian tribal communities in the Lower 48.

Public safety concerns over limited resources are severe across Indian Country, but disproportionately so in Alaska Native Villages. The rate of sexual violence victimization among Alaska Native Women was at least seven times the non-native rate. [5] On average, in 2003–2004 an Alaska Native female became a victim of reported sexual assault or of child sexual abuse every 29.8 hours. The isolation of villages and the inability to easily access tribal communities further create vulnerabilities of re-victimization for Alaska Natives. [5]

Given the national rates of crime victimization in American Indian and Alaska Native communities, it is necessary to address the resource parity for tribal nations. The Victims of Crime Act and the Crime Victims Fund is the largest source of federal funding for crime victims. While states and territories receive an annual formula based on funding from the Victims of Crimes Act (VOCA) fund, tribes do not. The BIA supports a tribal set-aside for Indian tribes to establish and strengthen victim service programs for crime victims in AI/AN communities.

In Fiscal Year 2014, $730 million was distributed from the Crime Victims Fund, and approximately $6.1 million reached tribes through tribal specific discretionary grant programs.

While these efforts are commendable, the level of funding distributed specifically for Tribes for AI/AN communities is less than 1 percent of the VOCA funds distributed each year. There is much more work to do to meet the critical needs of crime victims in Indian Country.

Unmet Needs faced by Tribes for AI/AN Communities

Designated funding specifically for Tribes for AI/AN communities would establish and/or strengthen justice for crime victims and meet some of the most critical and basic unmet needs in AI/AN communities. Crime victims in AI/AN communities have need for a wide range of services that are culturally appropriate and tribal specific. The proposed tribal set aside would allow Indian tribes to provide the following:

- Comprehensive community based programs to provide direct and immediate assistance to victims to include culturally appropriate crisis response and intervention, victim advocacy, financial assistance for emergency needs such as food and clothing, transportation, court accompaniment, and safe homes or shelters;
- Holistic services for abused and neglected children and children exposed to violence, such as Trauma Informed Care Centers and Child Advocacy Centers;
- Legal and criminal justice advocacy, such as initiatives to support local task forces and multi-disciplinary teams to improve child abuse investigations and prosecutions, forensic interviewing, and developing culturally specific models such as Sexual Assault Forensic Examination Support, Training, Access and Resources (SAFESTAR), to provide community based responses to sexual assault victims;
- Additional staffing for BIA Victim Specialist to serve all 26 BIA operated Law Enforcement Programs, and to expand the program to fund Tribal Victim Specialist positions to assist crime victims both in federal and tribal criminal justice systems. Tribes should be able to sustain not only human resources, but develop and enhance or expand current programs and services for the immediate needs of crime victims;
- Professional Development and Peer Mentoring across the Nation and regions to support advancement of tribal Victim Services (VS) programs, to identify and support new Promising Practices, to develop and expand Program Policies and Procedures, and to provide administrative and financial oversight of designated tribal VOCA programs; and
- Expanded National Data Statistics, Collection, and Research and Development Programs for Indian tribes.

---

[4] *Attorney General's Advisory Committee on American Indian/Alaska Native Children Exposed to Violence Report: Ending Violence so Children Can Thrive*, Final Report, November 2014.

[5] Indian Law and Order Commission Report, Chapter 2 *Reforming Justice for Alaska Natives: The Time is Now*, November 2013.

Tribal leaders and tribal organizations have advocated year after year on the need for change in the way tribes access funding to support sustainable victim service programs. Competitive discretionary grant programs are limited in capacity to provide sustainable victims services and resources for American Indian and Alaska Native communities. Due to the lack of adequate resources within tribal communities, once funding is unavailable, victim service programs lose continuity and often victims distrust the help that is available.

Conclusion

Tribes possess the ability to identify and understand the range of issues in their tribal communities; they are also closest to and understand what approaches are suitable and have the potential to create positive change. We must listen to the wisdom of Tribal Leaders and acknowledge our responsibility to provide Indian tribes adequate funding much like that afforded to states and territories. Tribes should be able to sustain not only human resources, but also develop or expand current programs and services for the immediate needs of crime victims.

The Bureau of Indian Affairs has the advantage of working alongside tribes and understands firsthand the severity of the lack of resources in Indian Country and the impact it has on tribal communities. A tribal set-aside for Indian tribes to establish and strengthen victim service programs for crime victims in AI/AN communities would help address this critical need.

The CHAIRMAN. Thank you, Mr. Director.
Chairman Stafne?

STATEMENT OF HON. A.T. "RUSTY" STAFNE, CHAIRMAN, FORT PECK ASSINIBOINE AND SIOUX TRIBES

Mr. STAFNE. Chairman Barrasso, Vice Chair Tester and Committee, I am A.T. Stafne. I am chairman of the Assiniboine and Sioux Tribes of the Fort Peck Reservation.

I would like to thank the Committee for inviting me to testify. I would like to share with you the considerable need for services for victims in Indian Country.

We face serious problems at Fort Peck. Our people continue to suffer from very high rates of poverty, high rates of homelessness and high rates of alcohol and drug abuse. All these are leading indicators of violence in the community. Unfortunately, violence is very prevalent at Fort Peck.

For example, in 2011 violent crime on the reservation was five times higher than the rest of Montana and almost three times higher than the rest of the United States. Roosevelt County, which covers most of our reservation, still has the highest rate of violent crime in Montana.

Domestic violence is a big part of the crime we must address. At Fort Peck, during one year from October 1, 2013 to September 30, 2014, our 911 call center received 718 reports of domestic violence. This means that almost twice a day, every day, our law enforcement officers are responding to a domestic violence call.

The rate of violent crime has serious consequences for our entire community. But what is most urgent for us is the impact that it has on our children. Violence accounts for 75 percent of the deaths of Indian children between the ages of 12 and 20. Twenty-two percent of Indian children suffer PTSD because they are exposed to violence.

In 2010, we had six students commit suicide and 20 more who attempted suicide. During that suicide epidemic, school officials reported that more than 30 percent of the middle school children tested positive for sexually transmitted diseases. At least 20 percent drank alcohol on a weekly basis.

These are children between the ages of 11 and 13. That is why I am here. We have to do more for our children. We have to find a way that we can help these children heal.

The Fort Peck tribes have taken a number of important steps to try and address the needs of the victims. For more than 40 years, we have had an independent court system. Our courts now have law-trained judges, law-trained prosecutors and law-trained public defenders. We also have probation officers and experienced court clerks.

Our tribal code and court opinions are published and available to the public. Our courts are supported largely by tribal funds. Because we want to combat domestic violence with every tool possible, we took steps to implement VAWA. We now exercise jurisdiction to prosecute non-Indian defendants who commit domestic violence on our reservation.

In addition, 30 years ago, we established the Tribes' Family Violence Resource Center. This Center is a primary resource for victims on our reservation. The Center provides crisis response and emergency services on a 24-hour basis to victims of crime and abuse. The Center helps victims with court proceedings and in finding shelter. It arranges medical care and provides counseling.

The Center works closely with police in responding to 911 calls. The Center provides services to any victim in need, whether the victim is female or male, Indian or non-Indian, adult or child. Most of the Center's work is done by volunteers.

The demand for services for victims at Fort Peck is staggering. In 2012, the Center provided service to 1,237 victims, both children and adults. In 2013, the Center provided services to 708 victims. In 2014, the Center served 886 victims. In short, over this three-year period, the Center was addressing an average of 79 victims per month.

This Center receives some support through the Justice Department's VAWA funding. We were also fortunate to receive some funding from the Justice Department's special Bakken Initiative grant last year. We are one of the few tribes to recently be awarded a discretionary competitive from the Justice Department's Office for Victims of Crime.

But apart from this recent grant, the tribe and our members have no assistance from the Crime Victim Fund. We need more help in order to serve victims in our community. Every year, the States receive a direct set-aside funding from the Federal Crime Victim Fund. In contrast, tribes must compete for grants. Only a few grants are awarded to a few tribes each year. And when the grant ends, the tribe must search for other funds to replace it.

Tribes need a consistent source of funds, so we can effectively run these victim assistance programs. Because of the need in Indian Country, we ask that Congress establish a 10 percent set-aside of the Crime Victim Fund for tribes. This request is supported by the Attorney Generals' Task Force on American Indian and Alaska Native Children Exposed to Violence. The Justice Department Office of Victims of Crime also recommended an increase in resources to tribal communities.

Although Fort Peck is dealing with some of the highest rates of violence in all of Montana, we have pulled and stretched together programs to help victims of violence. But it is extremely difficult to make the pieces fit together. We rely heavily on volunteers and short-term discretionary funds.

Our tribes have the capacity to address the problems. But our needs for victim services are overwhelming. That is why it is so important to create a more reliable set-aside for Indian Country.

In conclusion, I want to thank this Committee for holding this hearing on this very important matter.

[The prepared statement of Mr. Stafne follows:]

PREPARED STATEMENT OF HON. A.T. "RUSTY" STAFNE, CHAIRMAN, FORT PECK ASSINIBOINE AND SIOUX TRIBES

I am A.T. Stafne, Chairman of the Assiniboine and Sioux Tribes of the Fort Peck Reservation. I would like to thank the Committee for the invitation to testify, and share with you the considerable need for victim services in Indian country.

The Fort Peck Reservation is in northeast Montana, forty miles west of the North Dakota border, and fifty miles south of the Canadian border, with the Missouri River defining its southern border. The Reservation encompasses over two million acres of land. We have approximately 12,000 enrolled tribal members, with approximately 7,000 tribal members living on the Reservation. We have a total Reservation population of approximately 11,000 people.

The Considerable Need for Victim Services at Fort Peck

Nearly half of the people living on the Reservation are below the federal poverty level. Recent U.S. Housing and Urban Development (HUD) data shows that nearly 1,600 Indian families residing on our Reservation have household incomes that range from less than 30 percent of the Median Family Income to 80 percent of the Median Family Income. Homelessness is in excess of 10 percent. Further, Roosevelt County, where most of our Reservation is located, has the poorest health in the State of Montana. The bad health status is likely due to the rampant alcohol and drug abuse on the Reservation. Studies on the prevalence of violence in a community identify poverty, alcohol and drug abuse, and homelessness as the leading contributing factors to violence. Thus, it is no surprise that violence is so prevalent in our community.

The Fort Peck Tribes have provided law enforcement and correction services on our Reservation since 1996 under an Indian Self-Determination Act contract. We are also one of the first Indian tribes in the United States to enter into a cross-deputization agreement with state, county and city law enforcement agencies. Under this agreement, first ratified nearly fifteen years ago, tribal officers are deputized to enforce state and local law on the Reservation and state and local officers are authorized to enforce tribal law. Today, our law enforcement department consists of 18 police officers and 3 criminal investigators. This is approximately 50 percent of what is necessary to properly police a territory and population as large as our Reservation.

The violent crime rate on the Reservation in 2011 was five times higher than the rest of Montana and almost three times higher than the rest of the United States. Of the violent crime reported on the Reservation, almost 40 percent involved alcohol or drugs. We have also had to confront the plague of suicide that is devastating to far too many native communities. In 2010, we had six students commit suicide and twenty more who attempted suicide. There is nothing that tears at the fabric of a community more than when a child takes her own life.

While these numbers are staggering, they are far better than what they were in 1995 when the Tribes assumed control of the law enforcement services. At that time, the murder rate on the Fort Peck Reservation was twice that of New Orleans. Thus, while we have much work to do, I want to acknowledge that our law enforcement officers, tribal court and service providers have done a tremendous job in trying to keep our community safe for the last twenty years.

Unfortunately, we are again experiencing a significant rise in violent crime. We attribute the rise in crime to the rapid development of the Bakken oil fields to our east and increased drug use, in particular, heroin and methamphetamine.

In recent data summarized in the Montana newspapers, which ranked the level of violence within each county in the state, Roosevelt County ranked number one, the highest in violence, with Sheridan County ranking the third highest in violence. These counties comprise most of the Fort Peck Reservation. On the Fort Peck Reservation alone, there are 89 registered sex offenders. And in eastern Montana and western North Dakota (the Bakken region), there are a total of 392 registered sex offenders.

We are all too familiar with the statistics regarding domestic violence in tribal communities: approximately 34 percent of American Indian and Alaska Native women are raped and 39 percent experience domestic violence. In Montana, Indian women are 11 percent of the intimate partner deaths in the State. During a one-year period, from October 1, 2013 to September 30, 2014, the Roosevelt County/Fort Peck Tribes' 911 Call Center received 718 reports of domestic violence. This means that almost twice a day, every day, our law enforcement officers were responding to a domestic violence call. It is not known how many more incidents were not reported. What these statistics mean in real life is that one in three Indian women has experienced some sort of serious violent attack in their lifetime.

The rise of violent crime has serious consequences for our entire community, but what is most urgent for the Tribes is the impact it is having on our children. According to the Indian Tribal Trauma Center, Indian children are 2.5 times more likely to suffer trauma than non-Indian children, and violence accounts for 75 percent of the deaths of Indian children between the ages of 12 and 20. This is leaving a devastating legacy for our children. As stated in the November 2014 Report from the Department of Justice Task Force on American Indian/Alaska Native Children Exposed to Violence, Indian children experience Post Traumatic Stress Disorder (PTSD) at a rate of 22 percent. This is the same level as Iraq and Afghanistan war veterans. That means more than 1 in 5 Indian children in this country is suffering from battlefield-like PTSD. At Fort Peck, Poplar School officials reported to the Federal health team dispatched during the suicide epidemic that more than 30 percent of the middle school children tested positive for sexually transmitted diseases, and at least twenty percent drank alcohol on a weekly basis. Again, we are talking about children between the ages of 11 and 13. These are not independent, headstrong teenagers, these are babies.

That is why I am here. We have to do more for our children. We have to do more for the future of our tribe and our nation. We have to find a way that we can help these children heal. If we do not, my community and the rest of Indian country will be forever damaged.

The Steps That the Fort Peck Tribes Have Taken to Assist Victims

At Fort Peck, we have long believed that a strong tribal government is the way that we can best serve our people. That is why for more than forty years, the Fort Peck Tribes have had an independent judicial system, including an appellate court. It is through this system that we try to provide justice to our victims and our defendants. Our judicial system now includes law-trained judges, law-trained prosecutors, law-trained public defenders, probation officers, a published tribal code, and experienced court clerks and court reporters. Our court's opinions are published and available to the public. Our tribal courts and our court services—which are also essential to addressing the rights of victims—are largely supported by tribal funds.

Given the strong foundation of our court and the Tribal Council's desire to combat domestic violence with every tool possible, the Tribes elected to pursue the opportunity presented by the Violence Against Women Act (VAWA) and exercise our inherent jurisdiction to prosecute non-Indian defendants who commit domestic violence on our Reservation. We did this—not because we lack good partners in our U.S. Attorney and local law enforcement—but because this is simply another avenue to provide justice to the victims. We think providing justice to victims is an important step in providing them a pathway to heal and move on with their lives.

The Fort Peck Tribes were also recently notified that we are now a Substantially Implemented Tribe under the Adam Walsh Act and the Sex Offender Registry and Notification Act (SORNA). We have worked to achieve this status since 2009. Our ability to register sex offenders is another important tool in protecting victims and potential victims.

In addition to providing direct justice to victims, the Fort Peck Tribal Court provides other resources to victims. For example, we were one of the first Tribes in Montana to issue Hope Cards. The Hope Card allows someone, including a child, who has been granted an order of protection in one jurisdiction to easily prove it in another jurisdiction. These small durable cards, the size of credit cards, contain the necessary information regarding the order of protection for law enforcement to act. This is a small thing, but an important tool for our victims and law enforcement.

We have also worked to protect victims by establishing specific procedures to address their needs. For example, the Fort Peck Tribes are the only jurisdiction in Montana to have established a written Drug Endangered Children Protocol that sets out the responsibilities of social services and law enforcement entities for any scenario where children and drugs are involved.

Another critical step that we have taken to address the needs of victims was done thirty years ago, when the Fort Peck Tribes established the Tribes' Family Violence Resource Center. This is the primary resource for victims on our Reservation. The Center works directly with tribal, federal and local law enforcement agencies to provide services to victims of violence.

The Family Violence Resource Center is one of twenty-six domestic violence shelters in Indian country. The Center provides crisis response, emergency services and intervention on a 24-hour basis to victims of physical, psychological, economic and sexual abuse. The Center works closely with police in responding to 911 calls and in providing other emergency services to take care of the victim, whether female or male, Indian or non-Indian, adult or child, to be sure they are safe and healthy.

The Center also provides victims with legal advocacy services and assistance in connection with court proceedings. The Center's advocates work with prosecutors to keep the victim informed of offender charges, plea status, and release date for the victim's notification and safety. The Center's advocates also provide the victims with transportation to the prosecutor's office and courts when needed. The advocates also assist victims in filing for protection (restraining) orders and child custody, and by providing referrals to legal lay advocates in civil matters.

The Center's staff facilitates necessary health care for our victims, which includes accompanying sex abuse victims to medical exams to reduce trauma. The Center provides victims with shelter and safety plans, and crisis counseling (both cultural and secular based on the victim's choice). The Center operates a crisis hotline and provides community education. It assists victims by providing transportation to medical facilities, other resource agencies, and both local and off-reservation shelters when local ones are full or it is not safe for the victim to remain on the Reservation. The Center will also provide victims with replacement clothing and shoes when the victim's clothing has been confiscated as evidence.

The Center provides special counseling services, through a forensic interviewer/crisis counselor, for child victims and their non-offending parent or guardian. For those children who witness the violence, we treat them as victims as well and provide child friendly/age appropriate counseling services.

We recently moved the Center to a new facility, which we have named after Patty McGeshick (Red Bird Woman), a Tribal member who was a tireless advocate for victims, working any time—day or night—to ensure that a victim of violence had a safe place to be. Patty lost her lifetime battle with lupus this past year. She is deeply missed by our community, but her work continues through her dedicated staff at the Family Violence Resource Center and the staff at the Tribal courts.

The Need for Additional Resources to Assist Victims

The demand for services for victims at Fort Peck is staggering. In 2012, the Family Violence Resource Center provided advocacy and services to 642 adult victims and 595 of their children, totaling 1237 victims. In 2013, the total number of victims receiving advocacy and services was 412 adults and 296 children, for a total of 708 victims. In 2014, the Center served 519 adult victims and 367 children, totaling 886 victims. In short, over this three-year period, the Center was addressing an average of 79 victims of domestic violence and sexual assaults per month. The high number of victims served in 2012 reflects the significant impact that the Bakken oil boom had on violence affecting Fort Peck. With the decrease in oil production, we have seen some decrease in violence and crime, but every year brings new challenges. These now include meth and other drug-related violence, which the Center's staff has found is more dangerous and leads to long-term damaging victimization. Compounded by our proximity to the oil development activity, the need for victim services is greater than ever.

The work of the Family Violence Resource Center receives some support through the Department of Justice Office on Violence Against Women (OVW) Coordinated Tribal Assistance Tribal Governments Grant. We were also fortunate to receive some additional funding from the Department of Justice's Special Bakken initiative grant awarded last year. This one-time initiative focuses on training for area law enforcement, advocates and victims' service providers in the greater Bakken region encompassing eastern Montana and western North Dakota. The Center works hard to compete for grant funds each year in order to support its operations.

Much of the work of the Family Violence Resource Center depends on help from volunteers. The Center currently has five volunteer advocates who respond to domestic violence across the Reservation, and are on the weekend call list at the 911 Center. But while these volunteer advocates work without pay, they, like all other Center staff, must receive 40 hours of training before they can respond to the crimes of domestic violence and sexual assault. The Center must fund the cost of training as well as the related expenses that volunteers incur (such as costs of providing transportation) to provide services to victims.

Unfortunately, due to funding constraints, combined with the extensive need for victims' assistance, we handle virtually every case as a crisis and do not have the luxury of providing systemic and sustained support to our victims. The Center struggles to meet the need. When the Center itself does not have the resources, the Center's dedicated staff will use their own funds to help victims—to do simple but critically important things, like buy food and baby formula so the victim can feed her children while they travel to a shelter or while they wait for other resources to become available.

We are one of the few Tribes in the country to recently be awarded a discretionary competitive grant from the Department of Justice's Office for Victims of Crime. Under this grant, the Tribes conduct community education programs to encourage victims of sexual assault to report crimes and seek assistance. With this funding, we were also able to hire a tribal prosecutor to register sex offenders and establish a crisis hotline for victims. But apart from this recent grant, the Tribes and our members have not had assistance from the Crime Victims Fund. The victims we serve do not have access to other victims' resources. There has been only two times where victims at Fort Peck qualified for crime victim compensation: one was to replace glasses that were broken during the domestic violence incident, and the other was monetary assistance with a funeral. Both incidents took place over 10 years ago.

We need more help in order to serve victims in our community. Unlike states, which annually receive a direct set-aside of funding from the federal Crime Victims Fund, tribes must compete for grants. Our experience with losing our SAMSHA suicide grant program, notwithstanding our overwhelming need, teaches us that federal grants are fleeting. It is critical that the Victim of Crimes Assistance Act be amended to provide tribes a solid and certain funding stream, instead of requiring tribes to compete for a limited allocation of funds from federal or state agencies, so we can effectively support our vitally needed programs. In 2014, States passed through to Tribes 0.2 percent of the funds they received, and only ten tribes received grant funds directly from the Department of Justice. Clearly, this level of funding is not commensurate with the level of need throughout Indian country.

The Department of Justice's own Office of Victims of Crime, in their Vision 21 Report, called on increasing resources to tribal communities "to ensure that victims in Indian country are no longer a footnote to this country's response to crime victims." Given the disproportionate need in Indian country, we specifically ask that Congress establish a 10 percent set aside of the Crime Victims Fund. This request is supported by the National Congress of American Indians and the Attorney General's Task Force on American Indian and Alaska Native Children Exposed to Violence.

Finally, I want to thank this Committee for holding this hearing on this vitally important matter. Although the Assiniboine and Sioux Tribes are experiencing some of the highest rates of violence in all of Montana, our Tribes have pulled and stretched together a decent response for victims experiencing or exposed to violence. However, it is extraordinarily difficult to make the pieces fit together and we rely heavily on volunteer services and time-limited discretionary funding. Our Tribes have demonstrated capacity over decades, but our needs for victim services are overwhelming and we think it is so important to create a more reliable set-aside for Indian Country. I would be pleased to answer any questions and to provide any additional information that may assist the Committee in its work to help us address this unmet need.

The CHAIRMAN. Thank you very much, Chairman Stafne. We appreciate your comments and your testimony.

We next would like to turn to Judge Dianne Barker Harrold. Judge Barker Harrold, please.

STATEMENT OF HON. DIANNE BARKER HARROLD, TRIBAL COURT JUDGE, PAWNEE NATION OF OKLAHOMA; MEMBER, CHEROKEE NATION VICTIM TASK FORCE

Ms. HARROLD. Thank you, osiyo. I am a Cherokee citizen and I thank the Committee on Indian Affairs for their interest, concern and commitment to the needs of tribes and their citizens.

I am a former crime victim from the 1970s, when there was no recognition of needs or services for crime victims. In the early 1980s, that began. However, now the needs for crime victims in Indian Country have yet to be adequately acknowledged, understood and addressed.

I have served crime victims for almost 35 years, including being an advocate, an elected State district attorney. Currently I serve as a training and technical assistance provider for tribal victim services, funded through the Office of Victims of Crime, and have been doing that since 2006. I also serve on the Cherokee Nation's Victim Task Force, created by Principal Chief Bill John Baker, and am the attorney for the Cherokee Nation Tribal Council and Chief Judge for the Pawnee Nation.

Drawing from these many years of Indian Country knowledge and experience and working with crime victims, I know there are many unique challenges and unmet needs for crime victims in Indian Country. Throughout Indian Country the need for assistance for victim service is extensive, in part because tribes frequently lack any form of victim services infrastructure. Where services are available, there are still major gaps.

Although domestic violence and sexual assault is often addressed, there are Native victims of many other types of crimes, which include child abuse, human trafficking, elder physical and financial abuse, homicide and property crimes such as burglary or robbery, as well as many others, which shows the need for support.

For example, victims may need medical attention and other culturally-appropriate services to address physical and non-physical injuries resulting from crime. If a homicide occurs, a home needs major cleanup. Victims of crime need advocates, emergency shelter, crisis intervention services, cultural healing practices. And they do lethality assessments and do safety planning with the advocates and victim services.

Because a lack of transportation is a common issue in tribal communities, especially in large tribal reservations and jurisdictional areas, transportation is also a need that needs to be met by victim advocates as well.

Other things needed in Indian Country include educating victims about criminal justice system court proceedings, how their case is being investigated, the status of the investigation, accompanying victims to court proceedings, assisting victims in creating victim impact statements for sentencing, working with survivors of homicide victims, including related cultural activities prior to funeral services and finding resources to pay for funeral and burial expenses.

Community outreach to tribal communities is another need. Truly, service to crime victims helps to provide justice for crime victims and offender accountability. All crime victims need ways to heal and recover from victimization. Non-Native counseling is not the way healing and counseling is conducted in tribal communities, which is another reason for the need for more crime victim services in Indian Country, due to the need for culturally appropriate victim services as well as cultural healing activities such as talking circles, smudging and brushing healing which are physical and emotional cleansing ceremonies, sweat lodges, healing in the arts activities are some examples that should be noted.

Tribal culture and tradition is unique with each tribe, which has their culture, tradition, history and historical trauma. To be successful in Indian Country tribes must be given the flexibility to incorporate cultural healing and culturally appropriate victim services.

Building a collaborative system with tribal law enforcement and victim advocates is also an important part of this process. I have provided training and technical assistance services to three tribes that have created that collaboration which benefitted victims.

Internal and external collaborations with tribes and service providers is needed to ensure that service providers understand tribal culture and deliver appropriate services with a holistic approach if victimization occurs in an urban area outside of Indian Country.

Tribes also need the resources and support to create criminal codes to ensure that crimes are addressed, create a tribal victim rights code and to create a tribal law that and protect crime victims by being intimidated. If tribes want to opt-in to implement the Tribal Law and Order Act, it would be a major cost due to the Act's requirements.

Crime victims in Indian Country are often hesitant about reporting crimes due to the fact that there are no victim services to assist them. I have had direct experience in the past with victims who didn't report that were victimized, and sometimes the offenders even killed a couple of victims so they wouldn't tell anybody.

There is also lack of knowledge and understanding that tribes are eligible for victim's compensation as another impediment to crime victims in Indian Country. Establishing State and tribal liaisons will enhance this knowledge and understanding and facilitate access to victim's compensation funds for tribal crime victims.

The Oklahoma District Attorney's Council has established a great cultural victim's compensation policy and has also established a very beneficial State-tribal liaison.

Criminal jurisdictions in different areas can impact Service to crime victims, such as Public Law 280 States, where States have criminal jurisdiction over tribes. So that is another issue.

There is a misconception and a misunderstanding across the Country that these tribes have lots of money, because tribes have casinos and people think that all the money put in gaming machines goes directly to the tribe but that is not true. There is truly a need. And as the Chairman said, from Fort Peck, there is higher poverty rates in tribal communities than outside Indian Country. High poverty and unemployment generally correlate with high levels of criminal activity. Indian Country is no exception.

The major gap is lack of available tribal funding to create and sustain tribal victim services programs. The Office of Victims of Crime is really the only Federal agency that provides specific funding to fund tribal victims services. They are very dedicated. Director Joye Frost is very committed to serving Indian Country. Back in the late 1700s, Chief Tecumseh of Shawnee Nation said "Abuse no one and no thing, for abuse turns the wise ones to fools and robs the spirit of vision." So there was even a concept about abuse way back.

It has been an honor and a privilege to be able to provide this testimony. I thank you for your commitment to Indian Country. I want to say wado, which is thank you in Cherokee. As a Cherokee prayer blessing, may the warm winds of heaven blow softly upon your house, may the Great Spirit bless all who enter there, may your moccasins make happy tracks in many snows and may the rainbow always touch your shoulder. In Cherokee, there is no word for good-bye. It is only until we meet again: [phrase in native language.]

[The prepared statement of Judge Harrold follows:]

PREPARED STATEMENT OF HON. DIANNE BARKER HARROLD, TRIBAL COURT JUDGE, PAWNEE NATION OF OKLAHOMA; MEMBER, CHEROKEE NATION VICTIM TASK FORCE

Osiyo (Hello in Cherokee) to everyone who is here today and I want to thank Chairman Barrasso, Vice Chairman Tester, my Oklahoma Senator Lankford and this Senate Committee on Indian Affairs for their interest and concerns and commitment to the needs of tribes and their citizens.

I am a citizen of the Cherokee Nation, was raised by a Cherokee historian and have always been involved in tribal culture and have lived within the jurisdiction of the Cherokee Nation my entire life and am the mother of 3 Cherokee children and grandmother of 13 Cherokee grandchildren and 2 Cherokee great-grand-children. My grandfather was a full blood who received an allotment which is still within the family in Oklahoma. I am a former crime victim from the 70s when there was no recognition of needs and no services for crime victims. In the early 80's recognition of the needs and services for crime victims began and has continued to be more recognized since then. However, the needs for crime victims in Indian Country have yet to be adequately acknowledged, understood and addressed.

I have served crime victims for almost 35 years in a number of ways as an advocate, an elected state district attorney, a tribal court judge, managing grants to serve crime victims for a tribe and as an Indian Country expert and consultant. I created a video project about victim services related to homicide in Indian Country and I have provided trainings for victim advocates and law enforcement in Indian Country. Currently, I serve as a training and technical assistance provider for tribal victim services funded through the Office for Victims of Crime and have been doing that since 2006. I also serve on the Cherokee Nation's Victim Task Force created by Principal Chief Bill John Baker, am the attorney for the Cherokee Nation Tribal Council and Chief Judge for the Pawnee Nation of Oklahoma. Drawing from these many years of Indian Country knowledge and experience, I can tell you that there are many unique challenges and unmet needs for crime victims in Indian Country.

Many think of crime victim services as limited to legal advocacy, but this is not the case. Throughout Indian Country, the need for assistance for victim services is extensive, in part, because tribes frequently lack any form of victim services infrastructure and where services are available there are still major gaps. We must also overcome the misperception that only victims of domestic violence or sexual assault crimes require additional services. In fact, there are Native victims of many other types of crimes which include child abuse, human trafficking, elder physical and financial abuse, homicide and property crimes such as burglary or robbery, as well as many other which clearly shows there are crime victims in Indian Country in need of support.

For example, victims may need medical attention and other culturally appropriate services to address physical and non-physical injuries resulting from a crime. If a crime such as homicide, occurs at a home, major clean-up services may be needed. Victims of crime also need victim advocates, emergency shelter, crisis intervention services, emergency services and cultural healing activities. It is also important to allow for lethality assessments to determine risks and dangers of victims and create safety plans for victims to avoid re-victimization and assure protection from perpetrators.

Because lack of access to transportation is a common issue in tribal communities, especially in large tribal reservations and jurisdictional areas, emergency shelter and transportation services may be critical to crime victim safety and recovery. If a victim has no transportation, they often cannot seek assistance, go to court, obtain medical care or participate in cultural healing.

Other critical victim services that are desperately needed in Indian country include educating victims about the criminal justice system, court proceedings, how their case is being investigated, and the status of the investigation; accompanying victims to court proceedings; assisting victims in creating victim impact statements for sentencing; working with survivors of homicide victims (including related cultural activities prior to funeral services and finding resources to pay for funeral and burial expenses); and conducting community outreach to inform tribal communities about crime victimization and the services that are available. Truly, service to crime victims help to provide justice for crime victims and offender accountability.

All crime victims need ways to heal and recover from victimization. Non-Native Counseling is not the way healing and counseling is conducted in tribal communities which is another reason for the need for more crime victim services in Indian Country due to the need for culturally appropriate victim services as well as cultural healing activities such as Talking Circles, Smudging and Brushing healing which are physical and emotional cleansing ceremonies, Sweat Lodges, Healing in the arts activities which are some examples. It should also be noted that tribal culture and tradition is unique with each tribe who has their own culture and tradition, history and historical trauma. To be successful in Indian Country, tribes must be given the flexibility to incorporate cultural healing and culturally appropriate victim services for victims of crime.

Building a collaborative system with tribal law enforcement and victim advocates is also an important part of this process. I have provided training and technical assistance services to three tribes that have created that collaboration and victims have benefitted as a result. Internal and external collaborations between tribes and service providers is needed to ensure that service providers understand tribal culture and deliver appropriate services with a holistic approach if victimization occurs in an urban area outside of Indian Country.

Tribes also need the resources and support to create criminal codes to ensure that crimes are addressed, create a tribal victim rights code and to create a tribal law that would hold offenders accountable and protect crime victims by making intimidation of crime victims a crime in and of itself. If tribes want to opt in to implement the Tribal Law and Order Act, this will come at a major cost due to the Act's requirements.

During my years of experience, crime victims in Indian Country are often hesitant about reporting crimes due to the fact that there are no specific victim services in their specific tribal communities and they worry about being intimidated by offenders and offender's family members to stop victims from pursuing offender accountability. This can have dire consequences. I have direct experience with several cases where victims have not reported crimes, offenders re-victimized or intimidated them and ultimately at least two of the victims were murdered.

There is also lack of knowledge and understanding that tribes are eligible for state victim' compensation and is another impediment to crime victims in Indian Country accessing the resources they need to become whole. Establishing state and tribal liaisons will enhance this knowledge and understanding and facilitate access to victim compensation funds for tribal crime victims. The Oklahoma District Attorney's Council has established a great cultural victims' compensation policy and has also established a very beneficial state/tribal liaison system.

Different tribal and criminal jurisdictions are an issue that can impact crime victims. Jurisdictional challenges relating to Public Law 280 (PL. 280) further complicate matters for crime victims in Indian Country. Public Law 280 (PL. 280) states are states that have jurisdiction on tribal reservations. Although those PL. 280 tribes in the lower 48 states may have tribal law enforcement, it is state and federal prosecutors and law enforcement are the ones who investigate and file those cases but there would be a need for those state agencies to collaborate with tribes to have a tribal victim advocate to work with those state entities to ensure culturally appropriate services for tribal crime victims are available. For the lower 48 non-PL. 280 tribes that have reservations and their own tribal jurisdictions there is tremendous need for victim services as well. A major gap is lack of available tribal funding to create and sustain tribal victim services programs. Alaska has a different type of PL. 280 jurisdiction which has more culturally appropriate services since many Alaska State Troopers are Alaska Natives but due to rural and remote villages, unique and significant gaps in services remain there as well. I have worked with several Alaska Native victim programs funded by grants over the years and am in Alaska at least twice a year; however there is another witness today who will be focusing exclusively on Alaska.

There is misconception and misunderstanding across the country that believes tribes have lots of money because many tribes have casinos and people think that all the money put in gaming machines goes directly to the tribe but that is not true. There is higher poverty rates in tribal communities than outside of Indian Country. High poverty and unemployment generally correlate with higher levels of criminal activity and Indian country is no exception which is another justification for the need of funding for victims services in Indian Country.

Even back in the late 1700s to the early 1800s a tribal leader spoke about abuse. "Abuse no one and no thing, for abuse turns the wise ones to fools and robs the Spirit of its vision." Chief Tecumseh of the Shawnee Nation.

It has been an honor and privilege to be able to provide this testimony and I am now available to respond to any questions you may have. WADO (thank you in Cherokee).

Cherokee Prayer Blessing: May the warm winds of heaven blow softly upon your house. May the Great Spirit Bless all who enter there. May your moccasins make happy tracks in many snows and may the rainbow always touch your shoulder.

The CHAIRMAN. Thank you very much, Your Honor. We appreciate your testimony. We look forward to the testimony in a little bit.

We have one more witness to testify, that is Mr. Gerad Godfrey, the Chair of the Violent Crimes Compensation Board in the Office of the Governor of the State of Alaska. Mr. Godfrey, please proceed.

STATEMENT OF GERAD GODFREY, CHAIR, VIOLENT CRIMES COMPENSATION BOARD; SENIOR ADVISOR, RURAL BUSINESS AND INTERGOVERNMENTAL AFFAIRS, OFFICE OF THE GOVERNOR, STATE OF ALASKA

Mr. GODFREY. Thank you. My name is Gerad Godfrey, I am an Alaska Native. My parents descend from two different Yup'ik Native villages in the Kodiak Archipelago. I am a member of the Native village of Port Lions Tribe.

I have spent many years living in Alaska villages and I have chaired Alaska's Violent Crimes Compensation Board for the last 13 years. Currently I am senior advisor to the Governor of Alaska on Rural Business and Intergovernmental Affairs. I thank you for allowing me to be here today to discuss this most essential topic of improving victim services in Indian Country and rural Alaska, which is often defined by villages, which I will speak to.

I, as does the State of Alaska, greatly appreciate the Committee's willingness to explore ways to improve victim services to the indigenous people of America. As this Committee is aware, Alaska has a substantial Native population, with 229 federally-recognized tribes, which represents 41 percent of all federally-recognized tribes in America.

During my tenure on Alaska's Violent Crimes Compensation Board, it has become clear to me that Alaska Natives are over-represented as victims or claimants as well as perpetrators, in comparison to the representation of the population of Alaska as a whole. They represent an average of 31 percent of crime compensation board claims in Alaska, which is nearly double the representation of the population of Alaska. Alaska has the unfortunate distinction of leading the Nation in sexual assaults, and this statistic is even worse when isolated to rural Alaska and villages.

While rural Alaska suffers from many social and economic challenges, such as epidemic drug and alcohol abuse, high suicide rates, a lack of economic opportunity, a lack of infrastructure, a lack of telecommunications, high cost of living and high fuel costs, there is no greater challenge and social ill than the high rate of violent crime in rural Alaska and inadequate crime victim responsiveness and services. It is critical and timely for policy makers at all levels of government to address concerns of crime and safety in Indian Country and rural Alaska.

The challenges that are faced in these areas are multi-faceted. It is important to highlight that our responses to these challenges must be well-informed, targeted and multi-faceted if those responses are to meet any tremendous needs.

Accessibility to common services, such as public safety, health and education are often lacking or insufficient in addressing some of the social issues people face in the villages of Alaska. Improving victim services is such a broad topic and it holds many layers of importance. However, we would be remiss if we did not drill down into the topic of victim services to identify the most significant and pressing safety concerns facing those who live in villages.

Sexual assault is one of the most pervasive traumas that residents of villages in Alaska face. The Alaska Victimization Survey reflects that about 59 percent of Alaskan women have experienced intimate partner violence, sexual violence or both in their lifetime. That is six out of ten women who experience violence of this sort. And in rural Alaska, these women often have nowhere to turn.

In communities without victim services, a victim of violent crime like a sexual assault, or the protective parent of a child that is the victim of sexual abuse literally has nowhere to turn to keep themselves and their families safe. No service is available to help them heal from the trauma. This lack of services and lack of ability to appropriately address and heal from trauma is a vicious cycle that leads to substance abuse, depression, suicide, increased rates of violence and often perpetuation of these violent crimes.

To appropriate support victims of sexual violence in Alaska villages, my recommendation is to implement known best practices, similar to those already in existence in urban areas throughout Alaska. To form multidisciplinary Sexual Assault Response Teams is the most highly effective response in providing necessary services to sexual assault or child sexual abuse survivors.

A brief overview of response is, after the victim reports to law enforcement, an entire SART team responds to the identified facility, likely a health clinic in rural communities. The full team is comprised of law enforcement, forensic nursing, advocacy and the Office of Children's Service if a juvenile is involved. The full team participates collaboratively, reducing the need for a traumatized victim to tell their version of events more than once.

After listening to the victim's account, a forensic nurse knows exactly where on the body to look to retrieve evidence, minimizing the trauma of a full forensic medical exam. Law enforcement has the information needed to begin building their case, with quickly securing an arrest warrant, and victims are linked immediately to necessary victim advocacy services, including shelter programs and counseling.

SART teams improve the services provided to victims of sexual assault, minimize the victimization of survivors and lead to greater arrests, prosecution and conviction rates, making it an effective model to employ to combat sexual violence and support survivors, while effectively impacting community safety. Replicating this response throughout rural Alaska is a challenge due to the resources and implementation. With additional support funds, this SART response can be implemented minimally on a regional scale, providing this high level of service to the best of our ability wherever possible.

Conversations with State and tribal leadership to understand the needs and desires of each community throughout Alaska would be instrumental in ensuring the services provided are essential and welcomed by community members. There exists components already throughout Alaska that with some linkage would meet one component of the team, and those resources are already in place.

For example, the VPSO program, which stands for Village Public Safety Officer program, would provide public safety for rural communities in the region through a diverse array of public safety functions and include more than just law enforcement duties and activities. The presence of VPSOs in rural communities has had a significant impact on improving the quality of life, health and safety in the villages. Most villages in the Tanana Chiefs Conference region, which is the interior rural part of Alaska, primarily the off the road system and it is compromised of 42 villages, do not have existing public safety services or infrastructure such as fire prevention and suppression, emergency medical services, search and rescue and law enforcement officers or facilities.

To highlight the gross lack of service available, I would like to share with you an existing scenario in Bethel, Alaska, which is the southwest rural part of Alaska off the road system. Bethel and the surrounding 56 villages is home to approximately 6,000 Alaskans. Bethel has staggering rates of sexual assault and child sexual abuse.

In Bethel and surrounding villages, there is on average one rape or child sexual abuse case reported every other day. The aggregate total of cases coming from this region is almost 40 percent of all Alaskan sexual assaults.

As of two weeks ago, victims of sexual assault or child sexual abuse in Bethel and the outlying villages, after reporting the incident to Alaska State troopers, were retrieved by plane from that village and the troopers often would be delayed in response due to weather on their flight into Bethel. They would be placed in a hospital with no advocate and receive no medical treatment or evidence collection. The victim was then told they had to fly to Anchorage to undergo the SART exam.

That is entirely unacceptable for various reasons. I would be happy to elaborate on it if asked.

This was the state of affairs as recently as last week. So this highlights how desperately vital victim services in rural Alaska are needed more than ever to keep individuals and families safe. An influx of funding could help build the services I highlighted, having an immeasurable impact not only to Alaskans today but to future generations.

Rape and violence are rising. It is to ensure that effective services are in place to support Alaskans that deserve to be supported and safe.

Submitted with my written testimony is a comprehensive overview by one of Alaska's tribal consortiums. While they do not represent all the villages and tribes throughout Alaska, their analysis and overview is applicable and not unique when applied to villages throughout all of Alaska.

In closing, I would echo my fellow panelists about how valuable a set-aside would prove in meeting the needs of Alaska Native victims and helping break the cycle that exists. Thank you.

[The prepared statement of Mr. Godfrey follows:]

PREPARED STATEMENT OF GERAD GODFREY, CHAIR, VIOLENT CRIMES COMPENSATION BOARD; SENIOR ADVISOR, RURAL BUSINESS AND INTERGOVERNMENTAL AFFAIRS, OFFICE OF THE GOVERNOR, STATE OF ALASKA

Rural Interior Alaska/Tanana Chiefs Conference Region

1. About Rural Interior Alaska/TCC Region

Tanana Chiefs Conference (TCC) is a regional Native non-profit corporation in the state of Alaska that provides health and social services to 42 villages in interior Alaska, 37 of which are federally recognized tribes. The TCC region follows the traditional boundaries of the interior Alaska Athabaskan people. The region is spread across about 235,000 square miles, which is equal to about 37 percent of the State of Alaska and just slightly smaller than the state of Texas, and about ten times the area of the Navajo Nation- the largest reservation in the lower 48 states.

The tribes in the region are Athabaskan Indian that range in population from 75 to 700 members. Most villages are along the major river systems of Alaska's interior and the distances between communities can be vast. A majority of the villages are only accessible by small aircraft, and sometimes by boats during the summer months. Seven of the tribes are on the road system, with travel time from Fairbanks ranging from one to eight hours. In some villages, road access is over very rough gravel that makes travel difficult and dangerous depending on the season.

The total population of Native people in the TCC region is approximately 12,000. About half live in the urban hub center of Fairbanks, with the remaining 6,000 living in rural villages.

The TCC region is made up of six subregions. The Upper Kuskokwim subregion contains the following villages: McGrath, Medfra, Nikolai, Takotana and Telida. The Lower Yukon subregion contains the following villages: Anvik, Grayling, Holy Cross and Shageluk. The Upper Tanana subregion contains the following villages: Dot Lake, Eagle, Healy Lake, Northway, Tanacross, Tetlin and Tok. The Yukon Flats subregion contains the following villages: Arctic Village, Beaver, Birch Creek, Canyon Village, Chalkyitsik, Circle, Fort Yukon and Venetie. The Yukon Koyukuk subregion contains following villages: Galena, Huslia, Kaltag, Koyukuk, Nulato and Ruby. The Yukon Tanana subregion is made of up of Alatna, Allakaket, Evansville, Fairbanks, Hughes, Lake Minchumina, Manley Hot Springs, Minto, Nenana, Rampart, Stevens Village and Tanana.

The economies in the region are predominantly subsistence hunting, fishing and gathering, and seasonal employment. Unemployment rates in the villages are high, at least quadruple the national and state rates. Many families live at or below the poverty level. The cost of living in villages is estimated to be 30–40 percent higher than the cost of living in Anchorage or Fairbanks. Accessibility to common services such as public safety, health, and education are often lacking or insufficient in addressing some of the social issues people face in the villages. In the winter months, harsh weather conditions (temperature extremes of -55) limit the availability and delivery of basic goods and services.

2. Law Enforcement in the Region: TCC's Village Public Safety Officer (VPSO) Program and the Alaska State Troopers

TCC's VPSO Program provides public safety for rural communities in the region through a diverse array of public safety functions that include more than just law enforcement duties and activities. The presence of VPSOs in rural communities has had a significant impact on improving the quality of life, health, and safety in the villages. Most villages in the TCC region do not have any existing public safety services or infrastructure such as fire prevention and suppression, emergency medical services, search and rescue, and law enforcement officers or facilities. Those communities that may not require or do not have the resources to support a full time VPSO still have needs for other public safety services including public safety education, Drug and Alcohol Resistance Education (DARE), emergency preparedness plans, home safety inspection plans, school resource officers, hunter's safety, emergency responses and officer presence.

TCC currently has unarmed VPSOs designated to 11 villages; Tanana, Eagle, Allakaket, Tetlin, Fort Yukon, Nulato, McGrath, Huslia, Galena Rover, Minto, and Northway. VPSO rovers serve the remaining communities in the region. The VPSO program works in conjunction with the Alaska State Troopers to meet the public safety needs in rural communities. Alaska State Trooper detachments or service areas are based out of the Fairbanks Trooper Post and the Bethel Trooper Post, both of which are significant distances away from the rural communities.

3. Rising Crime in the TCC Rural Region

VPSOs and Alaska State Troopers are doing a tremendous job given their limited resources and adverse working conditions. Despite their best efforts, crime is on the rise (or is likely being reported more with the increase of VPSOs) in TCC's villages over the past 5 years. Consistent with the trend, assault, homicide, sexual assault, harassment, burglary, and theft have all increased from 2013 to 2014. Of particular concern is assaults make up the majority of reported crimes, which means there is always at least one victim.

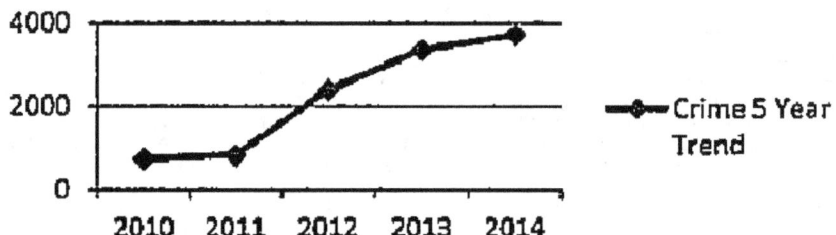

TCC Region
Crime 5 Year Trend

TCC Rural Region Crime Comparison of 2013 to 2014[1]

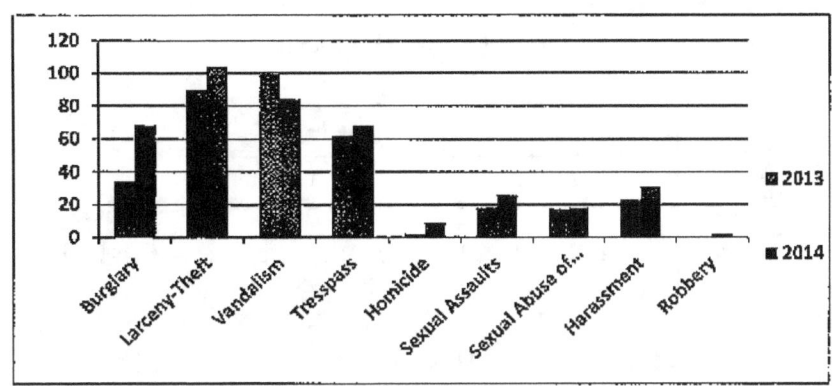

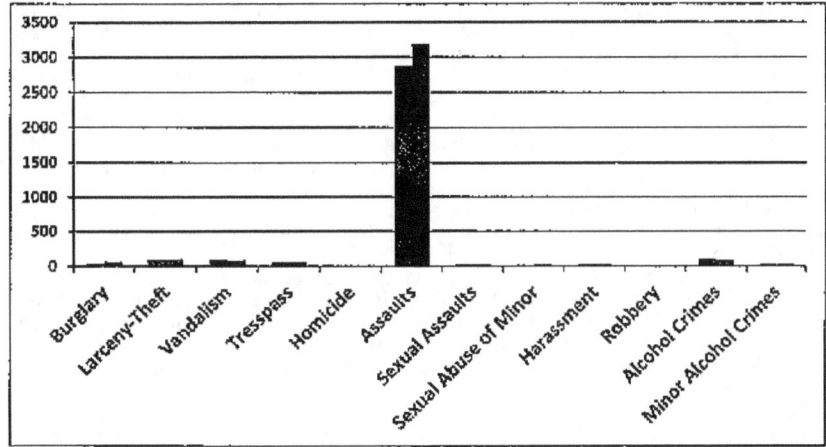

[1] Statistics refer strictly to the 6,000 people living in the TCC Rural Region and exclude Fairbanks, AK and Tok, AK.

4. Need for Victim Services in TCC Region

Victim services in rural Alaska are needed more than ever to keep individuals and families safe. An analysis of the statistics above is disturbing: In 2014, of the 6,000 rural residents residing in the TCC rural region, more than 3,100 incidents of violent crimes to the person occurred. Stated more bluntly, more than 51 percent of all people living in villages were victims of violent crimes. Looking at the other side of the coin is equally shocking: More than 51 percent of all people living the villages were perpetrators of violent crimes.

The causes for violence in Alaska Native villages vary. TCC VPSO Coordinator Sargent Jody Potts believes that law enforcement is dealing with the direct results of historical and generational trauma in rural communities. Children are being raised in environments where drugs, alcohol abuse, and violence are tolerated because offenders are not held accountable and victims have no access to meaningful services.

Whatever the core cause are, victims' service needs must be addressed now. First and foremost, every village resident must be protected. Every village must have a law enforcement officer present in the community. The TCC Five Year Crime Trend graph above indicates that crime has increased each year since 2010. What has also increased each year since 2010 is the number of VPSOs in rural communities. This statistic reveals that when rural residents have access to law enforcement in their community, they use it. When they do not have access, it is less likely that crime is reported.

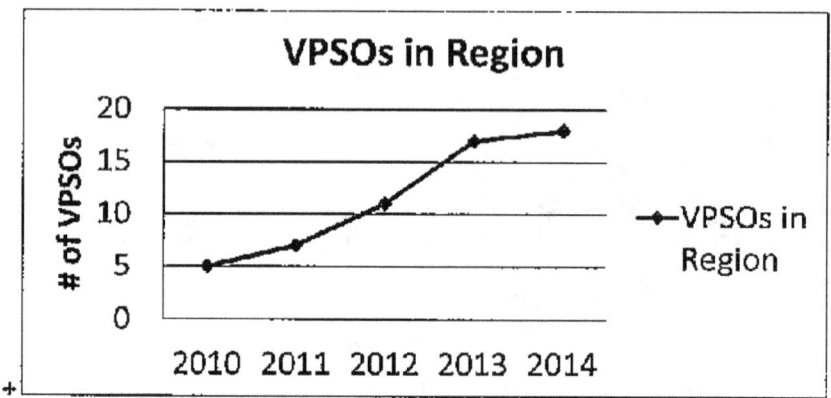

If law enforcement cannot physically be in every rural village, residents must have access to reliable telecommunication services to contact law enforcement agencies and emergency services. Many villages in the TCC region do not have reliable long distance telephone and Internet services. The only reliable telephone and Internet access are located in the village clinic or school. This does little good to a victim who needs immediate help and cannot access the clinic or school. This could be the difference between life and death. There should be no reason why rural residents cannot have the same access to reliable telecommunications in their home as the clinic or school located in the same community. However, due to various federal regulations that govern telephone and Internet access to health clinics and schools, village residents are prohibited from "tapping" into the same reliable access points.[2] This must be addressed.

Next, all individual victim focused services must consider the realities of living in an Alaska Native village and be culturally relevant. For example, in most villages, everyone knows each other. Victims may refuse medical care because the village's sole health aide is also the perpetrator's sister, mother, aunt, or other relative. Victims must have access to immediate medical care where they will feel safe and comfortable.

Victim retaliation and intimidation are other factors that must be considered. For example, a perpetrator or his family may retaliate by excluding the victim from necessary subsistence activities. This leaves the victim without valuable food resources for the winter and causes a financial burden because substitute foods must be purchased. The creation of a fund that helps cover the costs of subsistence activities by volunteers would be a way to ensure that victims still have access to subsistence foods while saving limited financial resources.

Lastly, in many domestic violence and other assault cases, perpetrators intimidate victims by refusing to leave the village or even the same home they share with the victim, while a criminal investigation is ongoing. Investigations can often last months. Victims have no choice but to stay in the same village or home because they do not have anywhere to go or the resources to support their children on their own. Creating and implementing services to victims must consider this reality. Collaborations with Tribal governments, Tribal courts, and law enforcement agencies are suggested when addressing this issue.

The CHAIRMAN. Thank you very much, Mr. Godfrey. We appreciate your coming all the way down from Alaska.

Senator Murkowski has come all the way from Alaska, and you are recognized.

---

[2] See FCC Rules, Regulations, and Orders administered by the Universal Service Administrative Company at *http://www.usac.org/about/tools/fcc/default.aspx*

STATEMENT OF HON. LISA MURKOWSKI,
U.S. SENATOR FROM ALASKA

Senator MURKOWSKI. Thank you.

Thank you, Mr. Godfrey, for your leadership in this and in so many areas. We truly appreciate what you have shared with the Committee on the issues that I think we recognize are beyond troubling. They take an amazing place, a great State, and bring us to our knees. We have to work on this, so I appreciate your leadership.

The CHAIRMAN. Thank you, Senator Murkowski.

We will now go to a series of questions. We will alternate each side and start with Senator Hoeven.

STATEMENT OF HON. JOHN HOEVEN,
U.S. SENATOR FROM NORTH DAKOTA

Senator HOEVEN. Thank you, Mr. Chairman. I would like to thank both the Chairman, well, first, I would like to thank all of our witnesses for being here and for your work. I would also like to begin by thanking both our Committee Chairman and the Ranking Member for their help in support in passing the Native American Children's Safety Act as well as other members on the Committee who co-sponsored the legislation.

What it provides is that for children in foster care on the reservation, background checks have to be done, not only on the head of household but on any adults in the home. We are working now to reconcile our version with the House. Representative Kevin Cramer led the effort in the House to pass the legislation there. So now we will reconcile the Senate version with the House version and it will go to the President for signature.

So this will become law. I want to begin by, in addition to thanking members of this Committee, I want to turn to Director Cruzan and say, one, tell me about your efforts to implement and make sure that this is enforced. Also, what are the steps you are undertaking to make sure that foster children on the reservation are protected when we do have incidents of violence and crime that we are addressing?

Mr. CRUZAN. Thank you, Senator. I am happy to report to you that we have been working very closely with the Department of Justice in West Virginia on this very issue.

There is a solution to this. And it is already in existence in a number of States. There are a number of States right now that are on it. The official title is called Purpose Code X. It is a data base system that is run through the National Crime Information Center. It is, in a nutshell, what the policy is, and we just implemented this, and we began in a small location and we will be working our way up.

But for that reason, and I have experienced this myself, you respond to a call at 2:00 o'clock in the morning, there is a parent that needs to be arrested for whatever reason. Social Services arrives and you are looking for somebody to come get the children. Oftentimes you are worried about putting them in worse situations, because Grandma shows up and Grandma is sober and fine, but you don't know who is in the home.

So through this Purpose Code X, we are now able to have Social Services contact a 24-hour BIA dispatch center, get those names run immediately. Similar to it would be if you were pulled over and your driver's license was checked. It happens literally that quickly. So we are able to feel more comfortable that we are providing a more safe location for these children, who are moving from a bad situation into a better one.

I hope that answers the question.

Senator HOEVEN. It does. But I also want to ask, what program or programs do you feel are most helpful for foster children to make sure that they are safe or in a situation where they have been victims of a crime, we have the means to address their needs and get them into a safe environment?

Mr. CRUZAN. I am certainly not dodging your question. That is an area that I think this Purpose Code X will allow law enforcement to feel comfortable in the emergent situation that is happening right now. I would probably defer that question to my counterpart in Social Services within BIA to answer that more in depth, how they are doing that through Social Services.

Senator HOEVEN. I would pose the same question to the other members of our panel. What program for foster children do you think is most effective in helping make sure that we address their needs and get them into a safe environment? Mr. Chairman?

Mr. STAFNE. I think you have to have trained personnel, social workers in BIA. But at Fort Peck, we have this Family Violence Resource Center staffed by volunteers around the clock. Every 911 call where there is violence or child issues, these volunteers go to the place where the call has been to and they meet with the officers. If they go to the hospital, they go up to the hospital to see the families. And they work completely with every department there to make sure that the children are taken care of. They have a list of all the houses or foster parents available to take that child immediately.

Senator HOEVEN. Ms. Barker Harrold?

Ms. HARROLD. As a tribal judge, I do a lot of child welfare cases. It is always important to know about who can provide foster care and be protective of children. Always, the basic need is the best interest of children and how they can be protected. Because a lot of times it is neglect or physical abuse, the reasons that child welfare cases occur.

So the need for making sure they are safe is a need.

Senator HOEVEN. Mr. Godfrey?

Mr. GODFREY. As far as an ideal model for foster children, while the need is ever-present in Alaska, and it is extremely important when dealing with trying to intervene and break the cycle of violence that is often the product of what leads to those children being in foster care, I am not an authority on that specific topic.

So I can speak to what is a good model or an ideal model. At this time, unfortunately, I can't answer that.

Senator HOEVEN. Again, I would like to thank the panel members for being here. Thank you, Mr. Chairman.

The CHAIRMAN. Okay, thank you. Senator Heitkamp?

Senator HEITKAMP. Thank you, Mr. Chairman.

I am horrified. Who could sit in this room and not be horrified. One out of almost every three children between the ages of 11 and 13 in middle school tested positive for a sexually transmitted disease on Fort Peck. In what world aren't we horrified?

Your testimony, Mr. Godfrey, I am horrified. I am horrified by all of this. Because somewhere along the line, Native American children are getting left behind. And they are getting left behind because they are in a jurisdictional juggernaut, many times, or they are in remote locations where it is very difficult to provide services, and where we don't fund what we need to fund to break the cycle of violence and abuse.

And so we worry about putting children in foster care. I worry also, in safe foster care, which is critically important. Why are they going to foster care in record numbers? That is another statistic that we haven't even talked about here.

So we need solutions. That is why Senator Murkowski and I have passionately shepherded a bill through the Senate and we hope it will get great traction in the House to try and find systematic response, some legitimate response. I can only tell you as an attorney general in the 1990s, these numbers shouldn't shock me. Because I saw the exact same thing in the 1990s. This is not a new problem. Suicide is a new problem and a new epidemic.

But what is a solution to a devastation of a human being. And you see it in these numbers. So I am here to ask you, just give us one idea, and we will start down at that end, one thing that would make a difference in the work that you do every day in trying to protect kids.

Mr. GODFREY. Probably the single most valuable thing is trained personnel to respond and intervene. That requires, predictably, funding.

Senator HEITKAMP. System funding.

Mr. GODFREY. Correct. And so while there are people who are willing to do that work and it is very, as one would imagine, very challenging subject matter to deal with, there are people willing to do it if the funds are there to train them and support them and help them be successful in what they do.

In Alaska specifically that requires teams that can mobilize on short notice in small planes to go to communities and villages that are only accessible by air or boat.

Senator HEITKAMP. I will tell you that through my work with Lisa, I can only say I thought my problems with remoteness were serious. I can't even wrap my mind around the problem that you have protecting a child in a village that is literally a three-hour plane ride away from any help.

Judge?

Ms. HARROLD. Remoteness is truly an issue in Alaska, because I do work with a lot of Alaska grantees. I go up there a couple of times a year. Still, the remoteness in rural areas in the lower 48 too are also an issue. Sometimes they don't get reported. So there continues to be abuse. Also, high suicide rates are becoming more common in youth in Native communities.

Funding is always a help for culturally-appropriate programs.

Senator HEITKAMP. And I want to conclude with the Chairman. Chairman, can you offer any suggestions?

Mr. STAFNE. Yes. I think you had the answer yourself. Consistent funding. With consistent funding, we would be able to track qualified people. No one wants to take a job where you don't know if after 30 days, 60 days, after six months or even a year whether you are going to have a job. If you do ride that out and last a year, maybe you get trained. And you get offered a steady job somewhere else.

Senator HEITKAMP. I just want to make this point to conclude, that it is ironic that when you look at what might happen in Williston or Watford City, you have State and local assistance. We are the primary. This government, the U.S. government, is primarily responsible for providing the network of support and the support services for Native American children.

And I don't know how you can listen to what you have told us today and what we know, what we hear over and over again, and not give this government an F in protecting the children in Indian Country. So we will continue to work to continue to believe that we can change outcomes if we all pull together for the children.

Thank you so much.

The CHAIRMAN. Thank you, Senator Heitkamp. Senator Daines?

STATEMENT OF HON. STEVE DAINES, U.S. SENATOR FROM MONTANA

Senator DAINES. Thank you, Mr. Chairman, for holding this hearing on such a critical issue.

Chairman Stafne, it is good to see you here today. It is great having the Office here as well, I am glad to have you as a partner working on behalf of Montana and on behalf of Montana Indian Country. We appreciate it. Thank you for your insightful testimony.

Senator Heitkamp expressed how I feel about these staggering statistics. The statistics you pointed out are equally frightening. On the Fort Peck Reservation you said that violent crime rates are five times higher than the rest of Montana, almost three times higher than the rest of the United States.

You also mentioned that Native children are two and a half times more likely to suffer trauma than non-Indian children and violence accounts for 75 percent, violence accounts for 75 percent of the deaths of Indian children between the ages of 12 and 20. This strikes home as a daddy of four kids. It is one thing to look at statistics. But each one of these children is a son or a daughter, a grandson or granddaughter, a niece or nephew of somebody that cares deeply.

So given these tragic statistics, how can Congress better work with tribes like Fort Peck to reduce the number of tribal members, especially tribal children, suffering from these physical and psychological traumas?

Mr. STAFNE. I think a lot of it has to do with what Senator Heitkamp said, consistent funding. We need qualified people to help. We can advertise a job, we hardly get any applicants, qualified applicants. We have to hire someone to train them. And once they get their training, they move on.

Senator DAINES. Is that because the offering salaries are too low?

Mr. STAFNE. Yes, I think so. The salary is lower, because we are trying to save money. We are probably using a grant. When that grant money runs out, we have no more money to pay that person. They move on. That happens all the time.

Senator DAINES. You mentioned a number of critical services which are currently available to survivors of physical or psychological, economic and sexual abuse. What services don't yet exist that would help these victims in Native communities recover and return to health?

Mr. STAFNE. Oh, boy. I don't know. I want to say services where we could, I know they exist, but in our land they are non-existent, partially because we don't have the funding. Alcohol plays the biggest part in all these crimes, I think. If we could somehow cure our people of the alcohol problems, a lot of these situations would not exist.

Senator DAINES. Thank you, Mr. Chairman.

I want to shift gears here and ask Mr. Cruzan a question. I appreciate your being here today. I remember when you and I met over a year ago in my House office, we discussed a number of important issues regarding law enforcement in Indian Country. I have spent some time on our reservations across Montana, we have a lot of open positions, unable to fill them, for law enforcement. According to the Office of Personnel Management, completing a background check for one applicant under the BIA Office of Justice Services takes an average of 105 days. I know we talked about in some cases we will have men and women returning from Iraq or Afghanistan who have worn the Nation's uniform, have had security clearances and yet come back, they want to serve back in their home, Indian Country, and we have difficulty getting them cleared.

Additionally, we have been told delays to fill vacancies have taken as long as a year or sometimes 18 months. It looks like we have a serious need for efficiency improvements to improve on the process.

Where are we there? Can you outline the steps? What are we doing to try to reduce that time?

Mr. CRUZAN. Absolutely, Senator, thank you again for that question. The process now has changed, I think, since we spoke to improve the efficiency. Because of Indian preference that the BIA has, we are able to now what we call, I don't think our HR professionals call it this, but it is commonly referred to as direct hire. So if a Native American applicant comes in and says, I am interested in a BIA career, we ask for their resume, their form 4432, which is their Indian preference, 214, if they were in the military and their college transcript if they have them.

We can do a quick, cursory background check, provide that information to our HR and they can literally do a tentative offer within that week. There are instances now of employees actually working for us now that have gone through this process.

Another exciting thing that we have just sort of fleshed out with our Federal law enforcement training center partners and the Department of Interior HR and our own is we want the ability to make an offer, not wait necessarily for the entire adjudicated background to occur before we schedule them for training. So they can sort of run concurrent.

There is a risk there, if for some reason there were an issue in a background that they weren't suitable for law enforcement, we would lose that time and that money. But I am told it is only about 3 percent of the people who we hire who are through that background process that don't make it through the background check.

So I am excited about that. I am very anxious to see how that works out.

The issue with the veterans, to me, honestly, we haven't gotten an answer that we want. We do think that these men and women who are serving in higher percentages in Indian Country, coming home, who have backgrounds cleared, we would be very interested in discussing ways for them to transition.

Senator DAINES. I would hope so. We have these programs, Helmets to Hardhats, a way to hire veterans. They have put their lives on the line over in Iraq and Afghanistan, they have already been cleared with background checks. The problem we face is, if we delay that, our best people move on and find a different job. They can't just sit idle waiting for a background check. I know we have to strike that balance, but I am thankful for the progress being made. I would particularly like to see more progress on helping veterans returning here. They are great role models to bring back home as well.

Mr. CRUZAN. Thank you, Senator.

Senator DAINES. Thank you.

The CHAIRMAN. Thank you, Senator Daines. Senator Franken?

STATEMENT OF HON. AL FRANKEN, U.S. SENATOR FROM MINNESOTA

Senator FRANKEN. Thank you, Mr. Chairman, for this, and Mr. Co-Chairman, for this very important hearing.

I wish all of our colleagues in the Senate could be here. Those of us who are on this Committee know very well what Indian youth face in Indian Country. And Senator Heitkamp talked about the 1990s and all these different kind of pathologies existing then. Those are the parents now. And these things repeat themselves.

We talk about trauma. The trauma alters the way your brain processes things, makes it impossible or near impossible to do well in school. Chairman Stafne talked about alcohol. We know you said that 40 percent of the crime is drug-related.

You start thinking of all these, and when you were asked what could help us here, you said funding. Funding. And I think of where, and this problem of funding is right. You need to attract people to these jobs and have them be real jobs.

Doctors, when they get out of medical school, where do they want to go? They want to go to a big city emergency room where they can practice on a lot of people. I would think if you want to get to know how to deal with kids who have been traumatized that this is the place to work, this is the place to learn. And we need to fund you.

But if you look at all the different things we hear about here, we hear about, where does the problem start? What is the entry point? Jobs. Housing. How many of these crimes against these kids happen when there are multiple families living in a house? Anybody?

Mr. CRUZAN. Senator, I would say that would be a factor, certainly. I couldn't give you a percentage, but certainly, yes.

Senator FRANKEN. How much of it is involved with drugs and alcohol? These kids, we fail them on just the schools, on teachers. We fail them, we fail Indian Country on law enforcement. We can't keep people in law enforcement there because they don't have housing. How do you attract someone to do this kind of job where there is not good housing?

In VAWA, we allowed, we gave tribal courts jurisdiction on assault, sexual assault crimes when the perpetrator is non-Indian. Chairman Stafne, it sounds like you have started to do that.

Mr. STAFNE. Yes, we have met all the requirements and we are utilizing that system now.

Senator FRANKEN. What is that experience like? Has that started yet? Have you prosecuted anyone?

Mr. STAFNE. We started, I haven't been over to the court, so I haven't heard. But that is probably good news. If it was bad, it would have come to me. The good news never comes. The bad news sure does, though.

Senator FRANKEN. Well, you get a lot of bad news all the time. So that seems to be working?

Mr. STAFNE. I think so, yes.

Senator FRANKEN. Well, I am glad we did that. I am a little like Senator Heitkamp, I will do everything I can to work with you and Senator Murkowski. I applaud you for your work on children. Thank you for traveling all this way to come here and tell us this. I wish I had something to say other than, as far as I am concerned, you can't get enough funding. We will do everything we can in this Committee.

But we need to talk to our colleagues who aren't on this Committee and don't hear this every week. Because they don't know, I don't think they know. Thank you.

The CHAIRMAN. Thank you, Senator Franken. Senator Lankford?

STATEMENT OF HON. JAMES LANKFORD, U.S. SENATOR FROM OKLAHOMA

Senator LANKFORD. Thank you. I thank all of you for being here and being part of this conversation. What you bring to it is incredibly painful. Judge, it is great to see you. It is always nice to have another Oklahoma face around, and to be able to have what you have done, and in your incredibly busy schedule, one that has you traveling all over the Country, contributing and working on these issues. Thanks for making time to be here and to be able to contribute to this conversation as well. Thank you for all your service there.

Ms. HARROLD. And thank you for serving on this Committee. On behalf of all the tribes in Oklahoma, we appreciate your service here.

Senator LANKFORD. Thank you. Let's talk about some success stories. That is one of the things I like to come back to. There are 566 tribes around the Country. My question is, who have you heard of that is having success in dealing with these issues? What are they doing and who is seeing a percentage drop in abuse? What do you see that is unique there?

I am confident we have several good success stories. Is there anyone who wants to jump in on that of any of the areas?

Mr. CRUZAN. Senator, I am happy to do that. Speaking specifically about violent crime, we did. We have been saying for a long time, if adequately resourced in Indian Country, we could have a significant impact on violent crime. This is going back to 2010 and current, so I will be brief.

The high priority performance goal initiative was to reduce violent crime by a percentage, 5 was the number over a 24-month period. The initiative was very simple: increased presence has a dramatic decrease on crime. As I was saying earlier, at the 12-month mark of this 24-month initiative, we saw a greater than 50 percent increase in violent crime, which was disturbing. But it wasn't until we began talking to tribal leaders that they said, it is not more crime that is occurring, it is more crime that is being reported, because there are resources out there to do something about it.

So four years later, we continue at those locations to see crime below where it was at that time. The initiative we are doing now, as the Chairman said, we see that as well. Alcohol and drug abuse is a huge problem.

Senator LANKFORD. Let me ask about that, because that has been a repetitive theme. Who has the most successful in Indian Country dealing with drug and alcohol issues? That has come up numerous times and this circles back to, as you said, not just a cultural issue or just an isolation issue, but a drug and alcohol issue as well. So that being a root cause, who is successful at that?

Mr. CRUZAN. I think there are some tribes in Arizona that do it well. Quite frankly, they have the resources to be able to. What we have in Indian Country are not violent offenders first. We have alcohol and substance abusers first who commit violent crimes. So some of these tribes that do have the resources to provide alternatives to incarceration, i.e., treatment, rehabilitation, I think are seeing some tremendous successes.

I could give you some specific names.

Senator LANKFORD. That actually would be helpful. You know Oklahoma well, also, and you also know what is happening all over the Country. So I am interested to know, where are we seeing success. We oftentimes talk about this as a problem, and there are serious issues.

But we have 566 laboratories all over the Country of different tribes that are actually engaged, that are trying it. And with some of them are success stories. I want to be able to isolate, how did they make that work, how did they make that connect. Sometimes that might be finances, sometimes it might be something else. I would be interested to know.

Mr. CRUZAN. If I may, I would be happy to work with you or your staff to get you specific examples and point to true success stories to potentially be pilots or models for us to follow in Indian Country.

Senator LANKFORD. Any other input from anyone on the drug and alcohol issue specifically, or other success stories on violent crime?

Mr. GODFREY. I will speak to both questions briefly. I can't speak to a model necessarily that I am aware of that is working. What I can do is speak to some of what I have observed in my time dealing with victims of violent crime in rural Alaska. The thing that is most effective is responsiveness and lack of responsiveness.

When I am thinking of with victims, and I will say victims of violent crime and then specifically sexual assault victims and sexual abuse of minor victims, is if they don't feel that what happened to them is serious and it was very bad and somebody cares, our opportunity to restore them emotionally, spiritually and mentally probably passes.

But beyond that, they also are more likely to perpetuate that as they grow older, whether it is a boy seeing Mom's boyfriend or husband beating her up when he drinks, but he only gets that way when he drinks whiskey and he only drinks whiskey once a month, so grin and bear it. That is acceptable behavior for him. But that a daughter would see that that is acceptable for her to be treated that way and stay in that household.

But that is a domestic violence. As far as the sexual abuse goes, same thing. If the message is not conveyed, that you're important, what happened is very serious and we are going to prosecute this person and we are going to get him in jail and then justice is served so the healing can continue to go forward and happen.

So what I see as most effective is highly-trained, highly-devoted response teams that get in there and respond. Sometimes it is law enforcement themselves that are multi-disciplined, because of being in Alaska and the rural nature of the State. I can't sit here and cite any program.

I can cite another thing that this board I chair has been able to do, and that is, provide some out of the box types of compensation for various types of recovery. We rely on a licensed therapist that is dealing with the victim to recommend for us and make their case, their professional case why this would be helping the healing of this child or this teenager. That has allowed us to do things out of the box. Our enabling statute in Alaska gives us the latitude and liberty to do that. But we don't come up with the ideas ourselves, professionals do. And they make the case, then we fund it.

One of my fellow panelists was discussing culturally-relevant healing. I couldn't agree with that more. In Alaska there are numerous culture camps. While it doesn't necessarily mean culture camp specific for victims of violent crime where children came from a family of alcoholism, it is the holistic approach of cultural camps and the spiritual and emotional and mental support and healing that takes place, and tying them back to the ancestral land and the ways.

Someone was talking about talking circles, all of those things. Technology is cut out. You go to a culture camp and you are isolated there with the elders and the wisdom that they share. And you do practices like catching animals, trapping, mending nets, fishing and other things that your ancestors have done historically. For a lot of these children that go there, and many of them go because they were, they had a scholarship or grant to do there, but it wasn't because they were a victim of crime. That stuff comes out when they talk about the abuse they are suffering at home. It is a catharsis.

That type of thing is out of the box, but it has a very high rate of success, when these kids feel valued and tied in to their culture and their ancestors and where they come from.

As far as alcoholism goes, in Alaska we have some villages that will vote to be dry or damp or wet. Basically that is three levels of prohibition or non-prohibition on alcohol. Obviously, if you are dry, it is hard to get the alcohol and consume it in the village without lots of planning in advance. And so I don't know that it resolves alcoholism, but it certainly takes away the implement, which is alcohol, that leads to very destructive behavior.

Senator LANKFORD. Thank you. I yield back.

The CHAIRMAN. Thank you very much, Senator Lankford. Senator Tester?

Senator TESTER. Thank you, Mr. Chairman.

I just want to thank you all for your testimony. It has been said before but I will say it again, I very much appreciate your insight into this.

Mr. Godfrey, thank you. You have talked about a number of things and I think the very first question that was asked, you talked about funding. Just now you talked about rapid response, which doesn't come without money.

Senator Lankford, I appreciate your line of questions about looking for success stories. I could almost guess that the success stories come with tribes that probably have gaming and probably have resources. That would be my guess. For those that don't, we have problems. And if we have ones out there that have success with the amount of money that we appropriate, I do want to see that, and I think we all would love to see that in particular.

If they are having success because of gaming and having those kinds of dollars, not everybody has access to those dollars. I can tell you, there isn't a tribe in Montana that has access to gaming money to the extent that it is going to a damned bit of good. So I appreciate your testimony.

I would ask you, Chairman Stafne, you said your police staff is about half of what it should be. I believe that is correct?

Mr. STAFNE. That is correct. That is information I got from our captain.

Senator TESTER. Do you have any idea, of those staff members, those police members you have, how many are funded by grants and how many are funded by the Bureau?

Mr. STAFNE. No, I don't. I could get that information to you.

Senator TESTER. And I don't expect you to have it, by the way. But I guess the question I have for you, Darren, when I point a finger at you there are three pointing back at me, so you know that. The question is, how under budget is your police staff for Indian Country. Chairman Stafne said he has half the number he needs. A fair number of those are funded by grants where there is no predictability. What kind of budget shortfall are we looking at?

Mr. CRUZAN. Yes, sir. The Tribal Law and Order Act requires BIA to provide Congress an unmet needs report. The last one that came out showed that about 48 percent met.

Senator TESTER. Forty-eight percent met. So for Chairman Stafne to say he has about half as many officers, he's above average?

Mr. CRUZAN. Yes, absolutely right. So I don't know his exact numbers, but it would not surprise me for that to be exactly right.

Senator TESTER. So as we look at this, and look, we are always worried, we will always need to continue to be worried about money that we appropriate and doesn't get spent in the right way. But in this particular situation, it would seem to me that if we gave you a few more bucks, we wouldn't have to worry about waste, because you guys are so damned underfunded right now that you can't get to where you need to be. Is that right?

Mr. CRUZAN. I am not sure how to answer that. I will tell you this, that being a good steward of the government's money is very important to me. Yes, I think it would be well spent and money well-directed.

Senator TESTER. And this is compounded because we are in a process right now where we are going to apply another round of sequestration to Indian Country and to everybody else that is not in the Defense Department. So things ain't going to get better for you guys, right? Is that what you would say?

Mr. CRUZAN. That is what I would say if sequestration, another hit would be coming, yes.

Senator TESTER. Okay. Well, we started this thing out in the opening statements, the testimony here is sobering. The testimony here is almost criminal, to be honest with you. We are right now with another generation in Indian Country. And I just don't think it is going to get better unless we give you guys the tools to make it better. Do you see another way?

Mr. CRUZAN. No, sir.

Senator TESTER. I want to express my appreciation to the Chairman for having this hearing. I also want to express my appreciation for the set-aside victims fund. It is at 5 percent; we can talk about where that needs to be and I don't know that we will get good metrics for it. Because if you guys have 5 percent of the crimes reported now, it is probably a heck of a lot higher if you were staffed up.

So it may have to be, we may have to try to arm wrestle the States for a few more bucks. But the bottom line is, I think the problem is even bigger than the Victims Fund. The problem is, we have to start a little earlier. I want to thank you, Judge, for the work you do. Mr. Godfrey, for your coming down from Alaska, I thank you very much. The testimony was incredible. You are answering questions, I really appreciate it.

And for A.T. Stafne, the Chair of the Fort Peck Tribe, who is probably going to hang his cleats up afterward, it is always good to have you here in Washington, D.C. You are probably just as happy to stay at home, I know that, because you live in a beautiful part of the world. But it is always good to have you here, Rusty, thank you.

Mr. STAFNE. Thank you. I enjoy working with people like you.

The CHAIRMAN. Thank you, Senator Tester. Senator Murkowski?

Senator MURKOWSKI. Thank you, Mr. Chairman. Thank you for calling this very important hearing.

I have been on the Indian Affairs Committee since I came to the Senate. And every few years we have a hearing very similar to what we have heard today. As Senator Heitkamp reminded us, this is not new. These are issues that we have been facing for years, perhaps just at a higher profile.

But Mr. Chairman, I really hope that as an outcome from today's hearing and what we have had put in front of us again and the statistics that we have been reminded of yet again about the horrible violent crime rates that we see among American Indians and Alaska Natives, two and a half times higher than national average, Native youth experiencing violent crimes at a rate of ten times the national average, we just say these statistics over and over and over again.

I at home remind people that our Alaska Native women are sexually assaulted at a rate of 12 times the national average. It is almost like you just become numb.

But think about those victims and how numb they are. Because in far too many cases, they have asked that their voices be heard, they have tried to speak up. But the services have not been made available to them.

In Alaska, we talk about the issues of jurisdiction and whether or not we have enough State troopers or whether we have the VPSOs and whether or not they should be armed. But you know, at the end of the day, and Mr. Godfrey, you spoke to this, we need to have rapid response.

But if the rapid response doesn't yield anything that equates to justice at the end, what have we done to let them believe that they do have value, that their speaking up will yield a different outcome instead of just yet another instance of victimization perhaps by the same person?

So if we look to the small things that we might be able to do to make a difference, prosecuting, well, you can't prosecute if you haven't collected the evidence, rape kits. I understand, Mr. Godfrey, that back home in the State, we have a backlog for rape kits waiting to be analyzed in the State, from the crime lab there, they say 150 plus backlog.

We have a lack of staff in the State, have a two-year training adding to the backlog. Sexual assault kits not tested on a first-in, first-out, but by most critical classification, leaving victims to wait. So you have a situation where even if you have gone to the extent to collect the evidence needed, you are not seeing a rapid response.

But even worse, I was at an event last evening talking about the situation out in Bethel. I believe you may have been discussing that when I came in, and I apologize that I did not hear all of your testimony. But I understand that in Bethel, YKHC has stopped collecting evidence from rape victims, or had stopped because of a funding issue. A community of 6,000 people, as you know, and the outlying villages, where there is nobody to collect the evidence.

So if you can't collect the evidence, there will be no rapid response, there will be no prosecution, there will be no justice for that victim. So he or she just gives up, just gives up, because we haven't been able to take the first step.

Mr. Godfrey, can you confirm whether or not we have resolved the situation in Bethel? Are they now collecting evidence from victims of rape? Have we addressed that?

Mr. GODFREY. Yes, Senator. The Governor's Special Advisor on Crime Prevention and Policy has dealt with that. The administration running the hospital has seen the light, if you will. Unfortunately, their problem had been one in which philosophically they made a comment and indicated that they thought that was a law enforcement function, not a medical function, so they don't know why they should have been doing them in the first place. But the trained personnel they had had moved on, and they didn't train up anyone else behind that, those trained SART response personnel.

Senator MURKOWSKI. May I just ask that question, then, the major hospital in the largest community in the region, you had one trained person?

Mr. GODFREY. Well, it has been resolved. All I know is the last, one of the last certified persons to do those tests has left the community. And they didn't train up anyone else. They have revised it now and have multiple that are going to be going through phased training, so they have redundancy in place.

But yes, there was a block of time and I don't know how long that was, where literally, if you had someone come in to do that collection, to do a SART exam, they had to go to Anchorage. And you hit on it, Senator, that is problematic for so many reasons, one of them being, the longer somebody waits to have evidence collected off their body the more degradation it goes through. So the less viable it is as evidence and more than likely, you don't make a prosecution.

The highest rates of recidivism in crime generally is the sexual assault perpetrator. That person is going to do that again, maybe that person they did it do or someone else or a series of others. So you really need the prosecution just for justice purposes, you really need it to help the victim get whole. But the message the victim gets, if you don't get them into a timely response, is my goodness, if you have a sexual assault victim that literally was just raped last night, and the first thing you tell them, well, don't shower, we have to collect evidence. And now you are saying, oh, don't shower for another 12 hours until we get you to Anchorage. But the only thing she wants to do is shower, obviously.

What is the message? What happens to their psyche? How are they going to heal and recover? And the despair that sets in, that is where the alcoholism and self-destructive behavior and suicide comes in. When that happens at a young age, and the message you get from the community or society or tribe is, you don't matter enough, what happened to you is not important enough for us to prosecute and put this person in jail or to get you the counseling and therapy you require to become whole again to try to start your life new and healthy again.

There are so many reasons that is wrong, when you can't have a SART team, from a psychological and emotional aspect, as well as the criminal justice aspect. And by the way, I would say that when a hospital says, well, it is a law enforcement function, not medical, many rapes involve blunt force trauma, contusions, lacerations, things like that, those are all medical. Those are all medically relevant.

I appreciate your taking specific attention on that, Senator.

Senator MURKOWSKI. It concerns me to such a great deal and again, the instance we are talking about is one of our regional hubs. We have so many villages, we have so many sub-regional clinics where we don't have trained personnel. We don't have the SART kits. We then have a backlog at the State.

We have a problem in our State, and I apologize to those who are outside of Alaska. I know you have been working this issue constructively. But we as Alaskans, at the Federal level and at the State level, must address these deficiencies that are so obvious and so glaring, where there is a solution. We have a lot of problems that extend from all of this. But if we can't give victims some level of certainty, some level of hope that their perpetrator is going to be held accountable, we are never going to make any headway.

Mr. Chairman, I have gone over my time. I would like to ask very quickly a question to Mr. Cruzan. This is based on the Committee memorandum that was distributed to us. In a footnote to our memo, it indicates that the President has proposed to divert money from the Crime Victims Fund to be used for purposes other than crime victim services without ensuring that even the most basic needs of crime victims are met and the continued viability of the services of the CVF. Why would they do that?

Mr. CRUZAN. Senator, I guess I don't completely understand the question.

Senator MURKOWSKI. Well, I didn't, either. I have been trying to get some more information about it. But basically what I understand is that it was in the President's budget that he sought to take money from the CVF fund to be used for purposes other than crime victim services. Now, we have talked about what can we do to make a difference. Unfortunately, so much of this comes back to money. Again, if there can be resources in the Crime Victims Fund, I would think that would help us.

So if we have funds that are in there, but the Administration has chosen to take them out to use them for other purposes, how can they do that, in light of everything that we have heard?

Mr. CRUZAN. Senator, I think that might be a Department of Justice question.

Senator MURKOWSKI. Will you look into it for me?

Mr. CRUZAN. I certainly will, yes, ma'am.

Senator MURKOWSKI. I think we all recognize that we don't need to be robbing from those very, very limited and meager pots of funding that could be used to help our victims.

Thank you, Mr. Chairman, and I apologize for going over.

The CHAIRMAN. That is quite all right, very, very important questions that need to be answered.

Mr. Godfrey, just to follow up a little bit on Senator Murkowski's questions, in your written testimony you said that more than half of all the people living in the Tanana Chiefs Conference Village are victims of violent crime, more than half are victims. And also more than half of all people in the villages are perpetrators of the crime. It is an interesting level of crime in the community to have more than half of both perpetrator and more than half as victims.

Based on your experience, do you think we could decrease crime, the victimization and the criminal behavior as well by expanding access to crime victim services or a better way to deal with this? It just seems an amazing situation at hand.

Mr. GODFREY. It is remarkable. And when you look at that, implicit in that percentage of victims and perpetrators is those victims become perpetrators, obviously. Intervention at a younger age and education at a younger age, especially in the isolated communities where it is harder for information and specialists and advocates in those fields to have a presence, a consistent presence.

I think a five-year old, four-year old, six, seven, eight, nine-year old, I didn't want to get into a policy discussion on this, but I think that if a child in that age range is educated about appropriate touch and inappropriate touch and what is acceptable and what is not, they don't then find it so easy to accept that behavior that is happening to them because an uncle or grandpa or their older brother or cousin or dad comes in their room once a week and does something like that.

I would think it is stigmatized in rural parts of Alaska the way it is at large. Nobody would ever want to be called a pedophile. And yet the stigmatization that I think we throughout the Country generally see when someone has that label, a child abuser or something like that, it is kept so quiet in rural Alaska. I have seen numerous instances where the victim, when she was 13 or 14, and this has been going on since she was 6, say, well, my mom walked in and saw my cousin doing it to me, but then she turned around and walked out. And another time she walked in and saw my grandpa, turned around and walked out. And one time I brought it up and she said, we don't talk about that. We don't talk about that.

I have also seen where an older woman told her child, it happened to me, it happens to all of us. That is not something you talk about. You just live, you will be fine just like me. And I am looking at those in police reports, when I am adjudicating these claims.

So I feel like intervening at a younger age, before it becomes not embraced, but tolerated by young children, that that is just the way life is.

The CHAIRMAN. The follow-up question is, Judge Barker Harrold, as you opened your testimony, you said that you were a victim and now here you are as a judge. Your written testimony refers to the risk of revictimization. I want to ask if you could describe in a little more detail how and why the gaps in victim services so often lead to this revictimization.

Ms. HARROLD. When there is not victim services people in a community, there is no one to help them. I have worked with a lot of Alaska Native groups. In remote villages in Alaska, for example, a lot of times those crimes don't get reported because it is a small village and sometimes they get intimidated by others that don't want to report it. Because going out to a remote village can take 24 hours or 48 hours depending on the weather.

But the same thing is true in a lot of the lower 48 as well, because if they know there is no victim services and no one to help them get protection, and it is not a negative to law enforcement, law enforcement is focused on arresting and investigating more than working with crime victims because of what they do, that would be a helpful thing to have, a collaboration, have an advocate work with law enforcement to have that.

But if people know that there are no services available, they are not going to repot it because they don't know how it is going to happen.

The CHAIRMAN. Senator Murkowski, did you have a follow-up?

Senator MURKOWSKI. Very quickly, Mr. Chairman. And it is a follow-up to a comment Mr. Godfrey just made about awareness and teaching children, our young people, about what is acceptable, what is not acceptable. A little bit of controversy right now in the State over legislation that is being considered. I know the Governor is very support of this, Erin's Law.

How important do you think legislation like that, that effectively puts in place sexual assault prevention education, so that we do have this awareness?

Mr. GODFREY. I think that is extremely valuable. I lived in Bethel as a child, I went to school in Bethel, I spent a number of years there. My father was a State trooper assigned to that post. I remember not learning about that good touch, bad touch stuff in elementary school there, when I reflect back.

But I do remember when I moved to the urban area, Anchorage area, that they did have that as part of the curriculum, a short thing. It wasn't in-depth. But I do recall that a very young age friends of mine, in third and fourth grade, making comments that just shocked me, because I was kind of naive. I was a kid, I was innocent.

And I asked a friend, why is your sister, because she had been held back from sixth grade, why is your sister so nice sometimes at recess, and then sometimes she just gets crazy for no reason? And he told me, I never forgot, because it was an eye opener for me at that age, he goes, she gets that way, her counselor said she's always going to be that way because a cousin and uncle raped her. So we just learn to put up with it. He was cavalier about it. And I was like, whoa, I have never known anyone who knew anyone that was raped before, in fourth grade. That wasn't as uncommon from that point forward in my life, living in Bethel.

But going to school, moving to the Anchorage area, I didn't have classmates talk like that. I didn't have classmates bragging about things they said they were doing that third graders wouldn't do. Maybe you would say that when you are in high school.

And then I moved to the urban area and my buddies were talking age appropriate. It was sort of strange.

I do know we didn't have that type of education in Bethel, and that type of good touch, bad touch or whatever you want to call the curriculum. But if someone doesn't illuminate for young children, this is not right, don't allow this to happen to you, someone shouldn't treat you this way, and they spend most of their time in a household and the message is, this is happening to me, this must be what happens, and they don't talk about it.

And by the way, Alaska Natives are culturally reserved people when it comes to communicating. So it is not like they are going to be predisposed to wanting to talk about it in any way. But if there is a cultural silence and keeping it behind closed doors, that is literally what they do. They leave the house and it is never talked about. When we go back home, that uncle, that brother, that grandfather, that father, does it. There are numerous victims I have come across that have been victimized by three or four different men in the community that she was related to. Those men typically were abused at some point when they were younger as well.

The only thing I see that would combat that short of having the police living in a household, which is ridiculous, is you educate these kids and counter the message, that message that is happening in the household, the message through actions. Obviously the father is not saying, this is what I am going to do to you, he does it. Counter that in the educational environment where the State has access and where the tribes may have access to those children to create some sort of tension between the action taking place in the household, behind closed doors, and what society should find acceptable.

Senator MURKOWSKI. Mr. Chairman, thank you for allowing me to ask another question. I think that given the statistics that we face in our State and really as you look at Indian Country across the Country, it would seem to me that we would be doubling down on our efforts to focus on the prevention, to focus on the awareness, as whole communities, starting with our young people, letting them know that this is not acceptable, that you do not have to tolerate that. And that it is okay to talk about it, because it is as we talk about it that the victims will heal and those who are perpetrators will know that this is not acceptable and it will not be allowed in our communities.

So there is a lot of discussion about whether or not we should require this in our schools. Until we can turn our statistics around in the State, I think we have to. Because in some of our small communities, where our school boards are making these decisions, it may be that some of those school board members are part of our problem. And they don't want to see these things, prevention, education, included in the schools.

It is one small thing that we can be doing.

Mr. GODFREY. Senator, if I may add briefly, you nailed it right there. There are people with a vested interest in a small community, because if they are not perpetrating it themselves, they know their brother or their husband is, or they have a family member that is, and they don't want that seen in the light of day, they don't want the troopers coming in and taking them.

My fellow panelists discussed that, the small community dynamic at work, even if I want to, even if you strike when the iron is hot and you want to get law enforcement and you get that person when they are willing to, the dynamic of familial ties in those small communities, often there are two or three dominant family names. And when you put report this person, half or more of that community will turn on you.

I have seen cases where moms or grandmothers say, if you report it, you know those families aren't going to take you to fish camp and they are not going to bring you berries in the fall. How are you going to feed the kids this fall when he is incarcerated if you do that? Using mental coercion and manipulation to keep them from doing that.

Senator MURKOWSKI. You are speaking truth.

Ms. HARROLD. One more thing about your question about re-victimization, Chairman, is that if an offender isn't held accountable, they think they can go ahead and keep doing that. So that happens a lot.

When I was a victim in the 1970s, I went through domestic violence for three years. There was no services or anything and I didn't know who could help. There was no shelter or anything like that, like the services there are now.

There is also years, centuries ago, many years ago where it was not uncommon for people, women to get raped or molested or something when they were younger, and then as they got older, those victims, sometimes they say to their children or grandchildren, that happened to me, you just expect to be raped at least once before you get 18. So sometimes that is a bad message because there has been no services to address those.

So that is different ways how revictimization occurs and having services, victim services in communities and tribal communities and people know that they are available, helps to give those victims a way to seek assistance and get relief and healing and hold offenders accountable.

Senator MURKOWSKI. Thank you, Mr. Chairman.

The CHAIRMAN. Thank you.

Chairman Stafne, you have been here listening to all of this. I just want to ask a question about your written testimony, referring to substance and alcohol abuse as major drivers of the significant rise in violent crime at Fort Peck and elsewhere. Are there specific services that you think would be most helpful in cases where the substance abuse is leading to part of this victimization?

Mr. STAFNE. Absolutely, yes. And we do have success stories, I guess. But they are rare. I get very discouraged at the number of people that go to treatment. As soon as they get out of treatment, or maybe that very night, we see them out there tipping the bottle again, probably with drugs. Drugs are more secretive, they are not like alcoholics.

But every once in a while you get a good report. And we are staffed by persons who have gone to treatment and that treatment finally took effect on them. There are good people working to get the other alcoholics or abusers referred to them, that they need to create a new life, a new life for your family, your children.

But it takes a lot of time, but we do have success stories, I am glad to report. We certainly employ the people, when they do come back, we try and give them gainful employment to help them. Sometimes it works. That is when it is a happy time, when you find somebody that it finally happens, and they realize that they need to change their life.

The CHAIRMAN. Thank you. I appreciate your testimony, all of you. Mr. Cruzan, let me finish with you. First, you may have noted previously, with other chairmen, we would have an Administration person come to testify and then so frequently they would leave and not hear this compelling testimony. I want to thank you for listening so attentively.

When Mr. Godfrey was talking, you were focused. I know it is not just you but your staff that is with you. I know you have taken these things to heart, what you have heard today. That is one of the things we have changed in this chairmanship, is to make sure that when people are here to testify, there is also an Administration person here at the table who will then stay to hear the stories that I think are so compelling. And you hear that from both sides of the aisle.

I don't if you want to reflect a little bit on what you have heard, what you are going to take away from today's hearing. I was impressed with how focused you were on listening to these three experts who know this better than any of us and had a message to share. I am glad that you and your staff heard it.

Mr. CRUZAN. Thank you, Chairman. I can sum it up in my philosophy. The people closest to the issues most of the time, almost every time, are going to know the solution, are going to have the solution to the problem, if the people in the positions with the ability to help will ask.

So I think that is what we do. I don't think it is a Federal Government solution alone, I don't think it is a State government solution alone. I don't think it is a tribal government solution alone. I think we are better when we work together. And that is the philosophy that we have.

I thank you for holding this hearing and I look forward to working closely with my partners here and the Committee to address this issue. It is without question, the Committee is on target. Victims in Indian Country and again, I don't need to tell you that, we have heard it, it is staggering.

I am very honored to have been here today.

The CHAIRMAN. I want to thank all of you for your testimony. Members can also submit questions, and that may occur as other members who weren't able to be here heard what went on today, they may also submit follow-up questions. The hearing record will remain open for two weeks. I want to thank all of you for your time, your testimony. The hearing is adjourned.

[Whereupon, at 4:10 p.m., the hearing was adjourned.]

APPENDIX

PREPARED STATEMENT OF HON. DARLA LaPOINTE, CHAIRWOMAN, WINNEBAGO TRIBAL
COUNCIL

Dear Senator Barrasso and Senator Tester:

On behalf of the Winnebago Tribe of Nebraska, I submit these remarks in advance of the Senate Committee on Indian Affairs' June 10, 2015 oversight hearing addressing the need for victim services in Indian Country. I ask for the support of the Committee in helping crime victims in our tribal communities get the services they need and deserve but currently lack. The Committee can do this by supporting legislative language to ensure an allocation from the Crime Victims Fund each year for federally recognized tribes. Doing so will make the Crime Victim Fund available to Native American crime victims, improving their life-chances and the well-being of their families and communities.

Adequate Funds Means Consistent Funds

Consistent as well as adequate funding is sorely needed to help crime victims and their communities in Indian Country. Unlike state and territorial governments, tribes can only access the Crime Victims Fund through state pass-through grants or limited grants from the Department of Justice. But last year the states passed-through less than 0.2 percent of CVF funding, and only to 20 tribes. With 566 federally recognized tribes in the United States, this meant that 96 percent of Indian Country lacked access to the Crime Victims Fund in FY 2014, despite its disproportionate need.

True, some tribes had access to other funds for victim services programs. We at Winnebago, for example, received CTAS grants from the Children's Justice Act Partnership for Indian Communities Program and from the Comprehensive Tribal Victim Assistance Program in 2013 and 2014. But those were the first such grants Winnebago had received since 1996, and even they did not address all of our needs. To be adequate, funding for victim services must also be consistent. Without regular and predictable annual funding, the benefits from assisting crime victims in one year will be eroded or lost in the next.

Current Need

The Winnebago Tribe is headquartered on the Winnebago Reservation in rural Nebraska, 20 miles south of Sioux City and 80 miles north of Omaha. Our 120,000 acre reservation is home to over 2500 tribal members, whose number is expected to double in the next 25 years.

Domestic Violence

In January of this year 10 cases of domestic violence were reported in our community in addition to 5 cases of sexual violence (not including incidents involving children), 3 suicide attempts and 4 sexual assaults. These are significant numbers in a community of our size.

Few things disrupt our hearts, our homes and our communities more than domestic violence, whose effects reach beyond its immediate victims. If forced to leave home with their children, survivors of domestic violence face immediate challenges like finding a new housing, getting a new job, and ensuring their children's schooling stays on track. These challenges are never straightforward, and can involve a host of smaller needs: What good is temporary housing without dishes in the kitchen or blankets on the bed? How are survivors of domestic violence expected to travel to new jobs, especially in rural Nebraska? How, for that matter, can they get their children to and from school without taking time off from work?

These are some of the victim services the Winnebago Tribe would like to provide to victims of domestic violence in our community. Right now we can't. At the moment we can only afford 3 staff members. Their dedication moves them to do double and triple duty sometimes, but also risks burning them out. Recruiting staff is also a challenge. Up till this year, the director of domestic violence services office had been vacant for two years.

Other services don't go far enough. Our transitional housing assistance is only available for 30 days. That didn't help one young tribal member who was forced from her home with her 7 children by an abusive spouse, and who had to spend two months in a nearby women's shelter run by a local ministry. Our current program also offers no assistance in things like the rent deposit for a new home or other basic needs like silverware, dishes or furniture, the lack of which can worsen the emotional stress of victims and their families and compound their suffering.

Culturally Appropriate Healing Services

At Winnebago, we currently have a single mental health counselor-therapist to serve our tribe's 2500-plus members. That's clearly inadequate, both for the community's needs and for the counselor's own well-being. As valuable as non-Native programs can be, they also often focus on the individual at the expense of the community.

In addition to the services of counseling professionals, we would like to see our victim services programs draw upon traditional spiritual resources. Sweat lodges, church support groups, ceremonials and other traditional practices not only help heal the individual victims, they help mend the fabric of our community tom apart by crime. The Department of Justice Office of Victim Services recognizes the importance of culturally relevant victim services, which have been successful throughout Indian Country. Funds should be made available not just to provide traditional healing practices like sweats and quilts, but to provide transportation when needed to make them available to those who need them. But again, given our rural location, transportation can loom large as an obstacle in implementing such programs successfully.

Conclusion

Establishing an annual tribal allocation from the Crime Victims Fund will guarantee consistent and adequate funding for crime victim services within Indian Country. Knowing funding will be available each year will allow the Winnebago Tribe to plan ways to better serve the victims of crime and build a stronger community for the long run. In the short term it could mean adequate staffing for existing programs and new programs for needs that urgently need to be addressed, like transportation; housing assistance; legal aid and counseling. In the long term, it would allow us to develop new programs that are consistent with our community's traditional practices and beliefs, like spiritual healing; counseling for staff members who provide victim assistance; family violence services; appropriate training for service providers; and assisting victims of crime from our community who have to navigate legal processes and social services in surrounding, off-reservation communities.

———

PREPARED STATEMENT OF JOYE E. FROST, DIRECTOR, OFFICE FOR VICTIMS OF CRIME, U.S. DEPARTMENT OF JUSTICE

Chairman Barrasso, Vice-Chairman Tester and distinguished Members of the Committee, thank you for the opportunity to submit a statement for the record on behalf of the U.S. Department of Justice regarding the need for improved victim services in Indian Country. I am Joye Frost, Director of the Office for Victims of Crime (OVC) within the Department of Justice's Office of Justice Programs (OJP). Our mission is to strengthen our Nation's capacity to assist crime victims and to provide leadership in changing attitudes, policies, and practices to promote justice and healing for all victims of crime. OVC administers the Crime Victims Fund, an innovative method for using fines and penalties from federal criminals to fund services for victims.

As the Committee is well aware, American Indian and Alaska Native populations suffer significantly higher crime rates than the rest of the Nation.[1] Both Congress and the U.S. Department of Justice have recognized these pronounced needs. OVC has long administered the Comprehensive Tribal Victim Assistance Discretionary Grant Program to help tribes or develop, establish, and operate multidisciplinary, trauma-informed services for tribal victims of crime. Through the Children's Justice Act, OVC also provides funding to tribes to improve the investigation, prosecution and management of child abuse cases.

Starting in Fiscal Year 2010, these two programs became part of the Department's Coordinated Tribal Assistance Solicitation (CTAS) which offers tribes a more

---

[1] *Criminal Victimization, 2010*, National Crime Victimization Survey Bulletin, September 2011, NCJ 235508 *http://bjs.ojp.usdoj.gov/content/pub/pdf/cv10.pdf.*

streamlined, comprehensive grant process. CTAS gives tribes the flexibility needed to better address their criminal justice and public safety needs. In Fiscal Year 2014, the Department awarded CTAS grants to 169 American Indian tribes, Alaska Native villages, tribal consortia and tribal designees. The grants provide more than $87 million to enhance law enforcement practices and sustain crime prevention and intervention efforts in nine purpose areas including public safety and community policing; justice systems planning; alcohol and substance abuse; corrections and correctional alternatives; violence against women; juvenile justice; and tribal youth programs.

Even with our long-standing efforts we know that victims in Indian Country remain chronically underserved.[2] That's why Indian Country is a key component of OVC's VISION 21 Initiative, a nationwide effort to expand the vision and impact of the victim assistance field in the 21st century. In 2013, OVC released *VISION 21: Transforming Victim Services Final Report,* the first comprehensive assessment of the victim assistance field in nearly 15 years. The report was a product of a broad spectrum of service providers, advocates, criminal justice professionals, allied practitioners, and policymakers who addressed crime victim issues through a broad range of perspectives.

The report stated that "Among those most in need of support are American Indians and Alaska Natives," and further emphasized "the urgency of finding ways to deliver services more successfully or, in the case of legal assistance, to deliver services at all. Complex jurisdictional issues, along with the cultural diversity of tribes and the basic reality of geography, pose a significant challenge. Rural Indian reservations may cover vast areas, and the villages of many Alaska Natives may be remote, even inaccessible, in winter." The report recognized the need to provide adequate support for victim assistance in Indian Country.

OVC has acted on the report's recommendations. In FY 2014, we awarded grants through VISION 21 to the Blackfeet Tribal Business Council; the Tulalip Tribes of Washington; and Wiconi Wawokiya, which serves the Crow Creek reservation, for tribal community wellness centers. These centers will go beyond the traditional model of victim assistance to draw on tribal culture and traditions in developing a more comprehensive community-oriented strategy. The strategy will include a full range of intervention, treatment, health and wellness, prevention, educational and economic development, and cultural resources.

In FY 2015 OVC issued a solicitation for the Vision 21: Tribal Victim Services Resource Mapping Project. This program addresses a critical barrier preventing tribal crime victims from receiving services—a lack of information. Our grantee will collect information about services available to American Indian and Alaskan Native crime victims at all levels, including tribal, state, regional and federal. The grantee will then develop this data into a state-of-the-art mapping and referral tool, which will be available to the public. OVC is also providing over $13.6 million in discretionary grant funding to tribes and tribal NGOs through CTAS in FY 2015.

Additionally OVC is directing over $830,000 to the BIA for victim assistance positions and almost $3.5 million to tribal NGOs to support training, technical assistance and capacity building this fiscal year. OVC continues to support numerous innovative demonstration projects in Indian Country, ranging from telemedicine to increase sexual assault victims' access to expert medical forensic care to mental health and culturally appropriate services for students in Flandreau Indian School to a tribal liaison project in Oklahoma that has increased the number of tribal applications for VOCA formula funding as well as compensation claims from tribal communities.

Through a statutory funding set-aside, OVC provides critical support to crime victims in Indian Country through FBI Victim Assistance Specialists, as well as staff in local U.S. Attorney's Offices (USAOs). In 2010, OVC increased funding to the FBI Office of Victim Assistance to support 12 additional positions in Indian Country; in 2015, OVC is funding seven additional positions dedicated solely to Indian Country and five positions dedicated to serving Indian Country part-time. OVC is also providing the Executive Office for United States Attorneys EOUSA funding this fiscal year for 12 additional positions specifically to serve Indian Country.

Our sister grant-making component, the Department's Office on Violence Against Women (OVW), also provides funding for tribes and victim services in Indian Country through three tribal programs authorized by the Violence Against Women Act and subsequent legislation. First, the Tribal Governments Program, which is administered through CTAS, supports tribal efforts to respond to domestic violence, dating violence, sexual assault, and stalking; enhance victim safety; and develop education

---

[2] *OVC Builds Capacity to Serve Crime Victims in Indian Country,* Office for Victims of Crime Fact Sheet, *http://www.ovc.gov/pubs/TribalVictimsofCrime/intro.html.*

and prevention strategies. Second, the Tribal Sexual Assault Services Program supports tribal services for American Indian and Alaska Native sexual assault victims. Third, the Tribal Coalitions Program supports the development and operation of nonprofit, nongovernmental tribal organizations that provide education, support, and technical assistance to member Indian service providers and tribes to enhance their response to victims of domestic violence, dating violence, sexual assault, stalking, and sex trafficking. In FY 2014, with funding from these three programs as well as other OVW programs, OVW made 91 awards totaling over $46 million to tribes and tribal organizations.

In addition, OVW provides technical assistance and training to tribes and tribal service providers to enhance their ability to serve victims of domestic violence, dating violence, sexual assault, stalking, and sex trafficking. Three of these projects illustrate these OVW-funded technical assistance initiatives. The National Indian Country Clearinghouse on Sexual Assault operates a website that provides a one-stop shop for information on sexual violence against American Indian and Alaska Natives and includes a toll-free helpline to provide personalized assistance to Indian Country justice and service professionals. The Southwest Center for Law and Policy's SAFESTAR project features a novel approach to providing sexual assault services in rural and geographically remote areas by training community-based lay health care providers (such as traditional midwives, medicine people, and community health aides) to collect and preserve forensic evidence in sexual assault cases, triage sexual assault-related injuries and health concerns, and provide referrals to sexual assault services. The Tribal Law and Policy Institute provides training and technical assistance to tribal coalitions to increase their capacity to address sexual assault and sex trafficking in their communities.

The Department also helps tribal victims of crime by implementing the Violence Against Women Reauthorization Act of 2013 (VAWA 2013), which is a high priority. A key provision of VAWA 2013 is the special domestic violence jurisdiction for qualifying tribes. The Department, along with agency partner the Bureau of Indian Affairs, has worked with tribes to help those seeking to assert jurisdiction under the "special domestic violence criminal jurisdiction." The effective date of the provisions authorizing qualifying tribes to exercise this jurisdiction throughout Indian Country was March 7, 2015. However, the Act provided for pilot projects prior to that date.

In short, the United States continues to prosecute domestic violence and violent crime in Indian Country—including the enforcement of the new VAWA 2013 assault charges—but it also promotes and encourages tribal prosecutors to bring domestic violence charges in their own courts when appropriate.

To that end, collaboration between the United States Attorneys' offices and tribal prosecutors' offices is continuous and essential. The Department's enhanced Tribal Special Assistant United States Attorney (SAUSA) program continues to be an important tool contributing to improved collaboration. Tribal SAUSAs, who are cross-deputized tribal prosecutors, are able to prosecute crimes in both tribal court and federal court as appropriate. These Tribal SAUSAs serve to strengthen a tribal government's ability to fight crime and to increase the USAO's coordination with tribal law enforcement personnel. The work of Tribal SAUSAs also helps to accelerate tribal criminal justice system's implementation of the Tribal Law and Order Act and VAWA 2013.

Our commitment to crime victims in Indian County and to improving tribal public safety and criminal justice comes through loud and clear in the FY 2016 President's Budget for the Department of Justice. It includes a 7 percent set-aside from OJP's discretionary funds to be made available for grant or reimbursement programs for flexible tribal justice assistance grants. The set-aside will provide a consistent source of significant, tribal-specific grant funding that can be distributed through a flexible tribal assistance grants model based on the lessons learned from CTAS. It will also allow OJP increased flexibility in awarding funds and streamlining reporting requirements. The funding provided by the set-aside will enable the tribes to focus on identifying their most important criminal justice priorities and developing innovative, evidence-based responses to address these priorities. Based on the funding levels requested in the FY 2016 President's Budget, OJP estimates that this set-aside will provide $114.4 million to support new and existing tribal justice assistance programs in FY 2016.

The FY 2016 President's budget also includes $20 million from the Crime Victims Fund for tribal assistance to continue and expand on our efforts to act on the VISION 21 recommendations. This would greatly enhance our work with our tribal partners and the OVW to develop evidence-based, culturally appropriate victims' services programs for the nation's tribal communities.

Furthermore, the FY 2016 President's budget requests $5 million for a new tribal Special Domestic Violence Criminal Jurisdiction program authorized by Congress in

VAWA 2013. This program would provide grants to tribal governments and their designees to support tribal efforts to exercise special domestic violence criminal jurisdiction over non-Indian offenders who commit violence against Indian spouses, intimate partners or dating partners, or who violate protection orders, in Indian Country. The Department needs this program to assist tribes in implementing the tribal provisions of VAWA 2013; the funds may be used by tribes to implement a broad range of criminal justice reforms, including updating criminal codes, providing counsel to indigent defendants, and supporting victims.

The Department of Justice, OJP, and OVC will not waiver in their dedication to improving the lives of crime victims in Indian Country, and we would welcome any discussion of how our efforts can be improved.

This concludes my statement, Mr. Chairman. Thank you for the opportunity to submit this statement on behalf of the U.S. Department of Justice.

————

PREPARED STATEMENT OF ROBERT STARBARD, TRIBAL ADMINISTRATOR/CEO, HOONAH INDIAN ASSOCIATION

Dear Chairman Barrasso,

Thank you for the opportunity to provide written comments regarding the Oversight Hearing on ''Addressing the Needs for Victim Services in Indian Country'' held on June 10, 2015. Hoonah Indian Association, a federally recognized tribe, respectfully requests that 42 U.S.C. 10602 (b) be amended to include, ''Federally recognized Indian tribes'' as eligible for the Victim Crimes Compensation fund. It is further our request that a minimum of 10 percent of authorized funds be Congressionally appropriated to American Indian and Alaska Native Tribal governments for the reasons described below.

A Change to VOCA is needed to Support Local Tribal Responses to High Crime Rates on Tribal Lands as Recommended by the Indian Law & Order Commission Report, ''A Roadmap for Making Native America Safer''

American Indian and Alaska Natives experience the highest crime victimization rates in the country.

- American Indian and Alaska Natives are 2.5 times more likely to experience violent crime than other Americans.
- Approximately 34 percent of American Indian and Alaska Native women are raped and 61 percent are assaulted in their lifetime. One some reservations, the murder rate is 10 times the national average.
- Due to exposure to violence, Native children experience rates of post-traumatic stress disorder at the same levels as Iraq and Afghanistan war veterans.

Despite these devastating rates of victimization in tribal communities, Indian tribes have largely been left out of the Crime Victims Fund (CVF), which is the federal government's principle means of providing resources for crime victims.

It is beyond debate that Alaska Native women are suffering extreme rates of domestic violence and sexual assault—rates that are disproportionately higher than that suffered by other women in the state and across the nation. There is much work that needs to be done immediately to combat this crisis, to protect Alaska Native women from violence, to increase and strengthen local life-saving services and justice to Native women survivors of this violence. Providing essential accessible resources to Indian Tribes that reach the villages in Alaska will account for successful and fair administration of crime victim funding. It is also crucial for the equitable distribution of life-saving resources to Alaska tribal governments.

Unlike state and territorial governments, who receive an annual formula distribution from the CVF, Indian tribes are only able to access CVF funds via pass-through grants from the states or by competing for very limited resources administered by the U.S. Department of Justice. According to data from the Office for Victims of Crime, in 2014, the states passed through $872,197.00—0.2 percent of available funds—to programs serving tribal victims. Of the 566 federally recognized tribes in the country, fewer than 20 received pass through grants from their respective state. It is painfully obvious that the current method of distributing federal victim services funding is not working for the 229 tribes in Alaska.

The competitive grants from USDOJ have been equally problematic. Fewer than ten tribes receive these grants each year for a three-year term, with no guarantee that this funding will be renewed. Unfortunately, without additional action by Congress, Indian tribal governments will continue to have no direct access to critical CVF funds.

Appropriate Funding is needed to provide adequate Native Village-based Services

The villages in Alaska experience high victimization rates, geographic remoteness, high poverty and cost of living, and an underdeveloped Alaska Native village-based victim services infrastructure that is the result of the historic exclusion of tribes from the CVF programs. While we know need is high, it is difficult to calculate the precise amount needed to fully meet the needs of victims in Alaska Native villages. Below are some examples of funding needs for tribal victim services and how CVF funds could be spent.

Tribal Domestic Violence and Sexual Assault Services

Native American women are assaulted at rates two and a half times the national average. Alaska Native women are disproportionately victimized at the highest rates across the country. According to the Indian Law and Order Commission report, A Roadmap for Making Native America Safe, Chapter 2, Reforming Justice for Alaska Natives: The Time Is Now, Alaska Native women are "over-represented in the domestic violence victim population by 250 percent; they comprise 19 percent of the population, but 47 percent of reported rape victims."

While some tribes provide services for domestic violence and sexual assault victims, resources for doing so are woefully inadequate. NEED: For FY 2014, the USDOJ's Office on Violence Against Women received applications from tribal governments requesting approximately $55.6 million for domestic violence and sexual assault services in its two primary tribal grant programs. OVW provided $33.26 million, suggesting an unmet need of at least $22 million.

Tribal Domestic Violence Shelters

There are currently fewer than 40 tribal domestic violence shelters in operation. In the State of Alaska, there is only one Native village-based Native women's shelter located in the entire state—the Emmonak Women's Shelter, which has been operating since 1979 and has been woefully underfunded. More often than not, the Emmonak Women's Shelter has not received federal or state funding and remained operational with volunteer assistance and donations. Those programs that do exist reported an unmet need of over 60,000 shelter bed nights in 2013. NEED: Building a shelter program in an additional 50 villages and tribal communities at a cost of $300,000/year would cost $15 million.

Sexual Assault Forensic Examiners.

The rate of sexual violence in Indian Country, including all of Alaska's tribes far exceeds rates of sexual violence in other communities in the United States. More than two-thirds of tribal lands, however, are more than 60 minutes away from the nearest sexual assault forensic examiner. With over 229 Indian tribes represented in Alaska, the vast majority of villages are located in the remote parts of Alaska where there are no roads; access is by boat, snow machine or airplane depending on climatic conditions. For Native women in Alaska, forensic exams typically are only located in hub regions, which means she must travel by plane to a major hub that may be over 200 air miles away. NEED: To fund one trained examiner in half of the 566 tribal communities at $50,000 for salary and benefits would cost $14 million.

Services for Sex Trafficking Victims

Sex trafficking victims need specially designed services, including victim advocates to connect sexually exploited youth throughout the state with culturally appropriate support and services they need; shelters and housing; and training for criminal justice and child protective services professionals who come into contact with such victims.

According to the State of Alaska Task Force on the Crimes of Human Trafficking, Promoting Prostitution and Sex Trafficking 2013 report, there is "a lot of gaps in information due to the underground nature of the crime and the tendency of trafficking victims not to self-report." Although lacking in data, the Task Force acknowledges that "trafficking have occurred (and likely are occurring) in Alaska, which is why the State of Alaska has gone to great lengths to create a task force to look at the prevalence of the crimes of human trafficking and sex trafficking in Alaska; the former Governor introduced an omnibus bill addressing trafficking (which strengthened penalties for trafficking); and in 2012 the Alaska legislature amended its sex and human trafficking statutes. NEED: To fund one trafficking advocate expert in half of the 566 tribal communities at $50,000 for salary and benefits would cost $14 million.

Services for the Survivors of Homicide Victims

Services for the surviving spouses, children, and other affected family members and partners of the victims of homicides are rarely funded but sorely needed. Between 2004–2007, Alaska Natives were 2.5 times as likely to die by homicide than Alaskans who reported "White" as their race, and 2.9 times as likely to die by homicide than all Whites in the United States.

Much needed services include criminal justice advocacy, assistance in applying for victim compensation, funding to travel to trials that are out of state, legal assistance, financial counseling if the murdered victim was the sole provider, mental health counseling or other therapy, and similar services. NEED: Iowa is the rare state that has committed to supporting regional services for survivors of homicide and other violent crimes. In FY 2014, the state used $393,441 in federal grant funds to support 4 regional programs for survivors of homicide and other violent crimes. Creating 25 such programs for tribal victims would cost approximately $2.5 million.

There is Wide Support for a Creation of a Tribal Funding Stream from the CVF

Last year, NCAI, the largest national organization of American Indian and Alaska Native tribal governments, adopted Resolution ANC–14–048 urging Congress to establish a 10 percent allocation from CVF disbursements for tribes.

Recognizing the disproportionate need for victim services in tribal communities, the Office for Victims of Crime's Vision 21 report also called for increasing resources to tribal communities in order to "ensure that victims in Indian Country are no longer a footnote to this country's response to crime victims."

The USDOJ's report on American Indian and Alaska Native Children Exposed to Violence similarly called for a 10 percent tribal allocation from the CVF in its 2014 report. A 10 percent tribal allocation from the CVF has also been supported by the National Task Force to End Sexual and Domestic Violence, a coalition of more than a thousand organizations that advocate on behalf of victims of domestic violence, dating violence, sexual assault and stalking.

Conclusion

No dedicated tribal funding stream currently exists under the VOCA for Indian tribes to administer programs to compensate and provide assistance to tribal victims of crime. This lack of funding to Indian tribes is unacceptable given the extremely high rates of violence including the severity of violence committed against tribal victims of crime. The USDOJ statistics document the well-known fact that violence against Indian women is more than double that of any other population of women; yet local services are lacking or do not exist in many tribal communities and Alaska Native villages. While states and territories receive an annual formula amount from the VOCA fund, the reality is that Indian tribes do not receive such an allocation and this must be remedied immediately. We urge an amendment to VOCA to direct 10 percent of the annual disbursement from the Crime Victims Fund to tribal governments. Thank you for this opportunity and for your leadership.

———

PREPARED STATEMENT OF HON. THOMAS RODRIGUEZ, CHAIRMAN, LA JOLLA BAND OF LUISEÑO INDIANS

Dear Chairman Barrasso,

Thank you for the opportunity to provide written comments regarding the Oversight Hearing on "Addressing the Needs for Victim Services in Indian Country" held on June ro, 2015. The La Jolla Band of Luiseno Indians respectfully requests that 42 U.S.C. 10602 (b) be amended to include, "Federally recognized Indian tribes" as eligible for the Victim Crimes Compensation fund and that a minimum of ro% of authorized funds be Congressionally appropriated to American Indian and Alaska Native Tribal governments for the following reasons described below.

A Change to VOCA is needed to Support Local Tribal Responses to High Crime Rates on Tribal Lands as Recommended by the Indian Law & Order Commission Report, "A Roadmap for Making Native America Safer"

American Indian and Alaska Natives experience the highest crime victimization rates in the country.

- American Indian and Alaska Natives are 2.5 times more likely to experience violent crime than other Americans.

- Approximately 34 percent of American Indian and Alaska Native women are raped and 61 percent are assaulted in their lifetime. One some reservations, the murder rate is 10 times the national average.
- Due to exposure to violence, Native children experience rates of post-traumatic stress disorder at the same levels as Iraq and Afghanistan war veterans.

Despite these devastating rates of victimization in tribal communities, Indian tribes have largely been left out of the Crime Victims Fund (CVF), which is the federal government's principle means of providing resources for crime victims.

It is beyond debate that Alaska Native women are suffering extreme rates of domestic violence and sexual assault—rates that are disproportionately higher than that suffered by other women in the state and across the nation. There is much work that needs to be done immediately to combat this crisis, to protect Alaska Native women from violence, to increase and strengthen local life-saving services and justice to Native women survivors of this violence. Providing essential accessible resources to Indian Tribes that reach the villages in Alaska will account for successful and fair administration of crime victim funding. It is also crucial for the equitable distribution of life-saving resources to Alaska tribal governments.

Unlike state and territorial governments, who receive an annual formula distribution from the CVF, Indian tribes are only able to access CVF funds via pass-through grants from the states or by competing for very limited resources administered by the U.S. Department of Justice. According to data from the Office for Victims of Crime, in 2014, the states passed through $872,197.00—0.2 percent of available funds—to programs serving tribal victims. Of the 566 federally-recognized tribes in the country, fewer than 20 received pass through grants from the state, and smaller, resource challenged tribes, such as those in California and Alaska, too often don't have the capacity to compete for discretionary grant funding.

The competitive grants from USDOJ have been equally problematic. Fewer than ten tribes receive these grants each year for a three-year term, with no guarantee that this funding will be renewed. Unfortunately, without additional action by Congress, Indian tribal governments will continue to have no direct access to critical CVF funds.

Appropriate Funding is needed to provide adequate Native Village-based Services

Tribes experience high victimization rates, geographic remoteness, high poverty, and an underdeveloped tribal-based victim services infrastructure that is the result of the historic exclusion of tribes from the CVF programs. While we know need is high, it is difficult to calculate the precise amount needed to fully meet the needs of tribal victims . Below are some examples of funding needs for tribal victim services and how CVF funds could be spent.

Tribal Domestic Violence and Sexual Assault Services

Native American women are assaulted at rates two and a half times the national average. While some tribes provide services for domestic violence and sexual assault victims, resources for doing so are woefully inadequate. NEED: For FY 2014, the USDOJ's Office on Violence Against Women received applications from tribal governments requesting approximately $55.6 million for domestic violence and sexual assault services in its two primary tribal grant programs. OVW provided $33.26 million, suggesting an unmet need of at least $22 million.

Tribal Domestic Violence Shelters

There are currently fewer than 40 tribal domestic violence shelters in operation. In the State of California, we have three Native women's shelters—operated by the Round Valley Indian Tribes (Mendocino county) and the Strong Hearted Native Women's Coalition (San Diego and Riverside counties). Those programs that do exist reported an unmet need of over 60,000 shelter bed nights in 2013. NEED: Building a shelter program in an additional 4 tribal communities at a cost of $300,000/year would cost $1,200,000.

Sexual Assault Forensic Examiners

The rate of sexual violence in Indian Country, including all of Alaska's tribes far exceeds rates of sexual violence in other communities in the United States. More than two-thirds of tribal lands, however, are more than 60 minutes away from the nearest sexual assault forensic examiner and transportation services are often limited, if available at all. For Native women in Alaska, forensic exams typically are only located in hub regions, which means she must travel by plane to a major hub that may be over 200 air miles away. NEED: To fund one trained examiner in half of the 566 tribal communities at $50,000 for salary and benefits would cost $14 million.

Services for Sex Trafficking Victims

Sex trafficking victims need specially designed services, including victim advocates to connect sexually exploited youth throughout the state with culturally appropriate support and services they need; shelters and housing; and training for criminal justice and child protective services professionals who come into contact with such victims. NEED: To fund one trafficking advocate expert in half of the 566 tribal communities at $50,000 for salary and benefits would cost $14 million.

Services for the Survivors of Homicide Victims

Services for the survivors of homicide victims are rarely funded but sorely needed, for surviving spouses, children, and other affected family members and partners.

Much needed services include criminal justice advocacy, assistance in applying for victim compensation, funding to travel to trials that are out of state, legal assistance, financial counseling if the murdered victim was the sole provider, mental health counseling or other therapy, and similar services. NEED: Iowa is the rare state that has committed to supporting regional services for survivors of homicide and other violent crimes. In FY 2014, the state used $393,441 in federal grant funds to support 4 regional programs for survivors of homicide and other violent crimes. Creating 25 such programs for tribal victims would cost approximately $2.5 million.

There is Wide Support for a Creation of a Tribal Funding Stream from the CVF

Last year, NCAI, the largest national organization of American Indian and Alaska Native tribal governments, adopted Resolution ANC–14–048 urging Congress to establish a 10 percent allocation from CVF disbursements for tribes. Recognizing the disproportionate need for victim services in tribal communities, the Office for Victims of Crime's Vision 21 report also called for increasing resources to tribal communities in order to "ensure that victims in Indian Country are no longer a footnote to this country's response to crime victims."

The Attorney General's Task Force on American Indian and Alaska Native Children Exposed to Violence similarly called for a 10 percent tribal allocation from the CVF in its 2014 report. A 10 percent tribal allocation from the CVF has also been supported by the National Task Force to End Sexual and Domestic Violence, a coalition of more than a thousand organizations that advocate on behalf of victims of domestic violence, dating violence, sexual assault and stalking.

Conclusion

No dedicated tribal funding stream currently exists under the VOCA for Indian tribes to administer programs to compensate and provide assistance to tribal victims of crime. This lack of funding to Indian tribes is unacceptable given the extremely high rates of violence including the severity of violence committed against tribal victims of crime. The USDOJ statistics document the well-known fact that violence against Indian women is more than double that of any other population of women; yet local services are lacking or do not exist in many tribal communities and Alaska Native villages. While states and territories receive an annual formula amount from the VOCA fund, the reality is that Indian tribes do not receive such an allocation and this must be remedied immediately. We urge an amendment to VOCA to direct 10 percent of the annual disbursement from the Crime Victims Fund to tribal governments. Thank you for this opportunity and for your leadership.

PREPARED STATEMENT OF CARMEN O'LEARY, DIRECTOR, NATIVE WOMEN'S SOCIETY OF THE GREAT PLAINS

Dear Chairman Barrasso,

The following are the written comments from our organization, Native Women's Society of the Great Plains, regarding the Oversight Hearing on "Addressing the Needs for Victim Services in Indian Country" held on June 10, 2015. As a tribal organization that works directly with tribal victim service providers and tribal programs who work with victims of domestic violence, sexual assault, stalking, dating violence and other crimes, we see the devastating effects these crimes have on women and their loved ones. For victims to truly heal, it is critical that they have access to culturally appropriate crisis and recovery services, which can be made available to tribes and tribal programs under funding provided by the Crimes Victim Fund (CVF). For the following reasons described below, we ask that the unmet needs of victims on tribal lands be adequately reviewed and considered as a matter of public policy for long-term solutions and strategy that ensure that tribal victims of crimes are able to access the CVF.

A Change to VOCA Will Support Local Tribal Responses to High Crime Rates on Tribal Lands

American Indian and Alaska Natives experience the highest crime victimization rates in the country.

- American Indian and Alaska Natives are 2.5 times more likely to experience violent crime than other Americans.[1]

- Approximately 34 percent of American Indian and Alaska Native women are raped and 61 percent are assaulted in their lifetime.[2] One some reservations, the murder rate is 10 times the national average.[3]

- Approximately 1 out of 10 American Indians 12 and older become victims of violent crime annually.[4]

Despite these devastating rates of victimization in tribal communities, Indian tribes have largely been left out of the Crime Victims Fund (CVF), which is the federal government's principle means of providing resources for crime victims.

Unlike state and territorial governments, who receive an annual formula distribution from the CVF, Indian tribes are only able to access CVF funds via pass-through grants from the states or by competing for very limited resources administered by the U.S. Department of Justice. The current method of distributing federal victim services funding to tribal governments is simply not working for the Tribes in the Great Plains area where the coalition's membership serve women. According to data from the Office for Victims of Crime, in 2014, the states passed through $872,197.00—0.2 percent of available funds—to programs serving tribal victims. Of the 566 federally-recognized tribes in the country, fewer than 20 received pass through grants from their respective state.

The competitive grants from USDOJ have been equally problematic. Fewer than ten tribes receive these grants each year for a three-year term, with no guarantee that this funding will be renewed. Unfortunately, without additional action by Congress, Indian tribal governments will continue to have no direct access to critical CVF funds.

Appropriate Funding Will Help Provide Adequate Native Village-based Services

Indian Tribes experience high victimization rates, geographic remoteness, high poverty and cost of living, and an underdeveloped tribally based victim services infrastructure that is the result of the historic exclusion of tribes from the CVF programs. While we know need is high, it is difficult to calculate the precise amount needed to fully meet the needs of victims on tribal lands. Below are some examples of funding needs for tribal victim services and how CVF funds could be spent.

Tribal Domestic Violence and Sexual Assault Services

Native American women are assaulted at rates two and a half times the national average. While some tribes provide services for domestic violence and sexual assault victims, resources for doing so are woefully inadequate.

Tribal Domestic Violence Shelters

There are currently fewer than 40 tribal domestic violence shelters in operation. Those programs that do exist reported an unmet need of over 60,000 shelter bed nights in 2013.

Sexual Assault Forensic Examiners

The rate of sexual violence in Indian Country, including all of Alaska's tribes far exceeds rates of sexual violence in other communities in the United States. More

---

[1] Rennison, C. (2001). Violent Victimization and Race, 1993–98. U.S. DOJ, Bureau of Justice Statistics, March, (NCJ 176354).

[2] Tjaden, P. & Thonennes. (2000). The Prevalence, Incidence, and Consequences of Violence Against Women: findings from the National Violence Survey Against Women. National Institute of Justice & the Centers for Disease Control & Prevention. *http://www.ncjrs.gov/txtfiles1/nij/183781.txt*

[3] Ronet, Bachman, et al, Violence Against American Indian and Alaska Native Women and the Criminal Justice Response: What is Known (National Institute of Justice 2007).

[4] 2004 report, American Indians and Crime, A BJS Statistical Profile, 1992–2002

than two-thirds of tribal lands, however, are more than 60 minutes away from the nearest sexual assault forensic examiner.

Services for Sex Trafficking Victims

Sex trafficking victims need specially designed services, including victim advocates to connect sexually exploited youth throughout the state with culturally appropriate support and services they need; shelters and housing; and training for criminal justice and child protective services professionals who come into contact with such victims.

Services for the Survivors of Homicide Victims

Services for the survivors of homicide victims are rarely funded but sorely needed, for surviving spouses, children, and other affected family members and partners. Much needed services include criminal justice advocacy, assistance in applying for victim compensation, funding to travel to trials that are out of state, legal assistance, financial counseling if the murdered victim was the sole provider, mental health counseling or other therapy, and similar services.

There is Wide Support for a Creation of a Tribal Funding Stream from the CVF

Last year, NCAI, the largest national organization of American Indian and Alaska Native tribal governments, adopted Resolution ANC–14–048 which supports an allocation from CVF disbursements for tribes.

Recognizing the disproportionate need for victim services in tribal communities, the Office for Victims of Crime's *Vision 21* report also called for increasing resources to tribal communities in order to ''ensure that victims in Indian Country are no longer a footnote to this country's response to crime victims.''[5]

The USDOJ's report on American Indian and Alaska Native Children Exposed to Violence similarly called for a tribal allocation from the CVF in its 2014 report.[6]

A tribal allocation from the CVF has also been supported by the National Task Force to End Sexual and Domestic Violence, a coalition of more than a thousand organizations that advocate on behalf of victims of domestic violence, dating violence, sexual assault and stalking.[7]

Conclusion

No dedicated tribal funding stream currently exists under the VOCA for Indian tribes to administer programs to compensate and provide assistance to tribal victims of crime. This lack of funding to Indian tribes is unacceptable given the extremely high rates of violence including the severity of violence committed against tribal victims of crime. The USDOJ statistics document the well-known fact that violence against Indian women is more than double that of any other population of women; yet local services are lacking or do not exist in many tribal communities and Alaska Native villages. While states and territories receive an annual formula amount from the VOCA fund, the reality is that Indian tribes do not receive such an allocation and this must be remedied immediately. We request a policy shift that will provide for, through an amendment to VOCA, an annual disbursement from the Crime Victims Fund to tribal governments. Thank you for this opportunity to present a summary of recent findings on this issue and for your leadership.

———

PREPARED STATEMENT OF HON. MICHAEL SAM, CHIEF, NATIVE VILLAGE OF TETLIN

Dear Chairman Barrasso,

Thank you for the opportunity to provide written comments regarding the Oversight Hearing on ''Addressing the Needs for Victim Services in Indian Country'' held on June 10, 2015. The Native Village of Tetlin respectfully requests that 42 U.S.C. 10602 (b) be amended to include, ''Federally recognized Indian tribes'' as eligible for the Victim Crimes Compensation fund. It is further our request that a minimum of 10 percent of authorized funds be Congressionally appropriated to American Indian and Alaska Native Tribal governments for the reasons described below.

---

[5] Office of Justice Programs, U.S. Department of Justice, Vision 21: Transforming Victim Services Final Report, (Washington, DC: OVC, 2014).

[6] Office of Justice Programs, United States Department of Justice, Attorney General's Advisory Committee on American Indian/Alaska Native Children Exposed to Violence: Ending Violence so Children Can Thrive.

[7] NTF Letter to Appropriators, April 15, 2015, available at *http://4vawa.org/4vawa/2015/4/21/ntf-urges-for-increase-funding-for-federal-programs-that-address-domestic-violence-sexual-assault-dating-violence-and-stalking.*

A Change to VOCA is needed to Support Local Tribal Responses to High Crime Rates on Tribal Lands as Recommended by the Indian Law & Order Commission Report, "A Roadmap for Making Native America Safer"

American Indian and Alaska Natives experience the highest crime victimization rates in the country.

- American Indian and Alaska Natives are 2.5 times more likely to experience violent crime than other Americans.
- Approximately 34 percent of American Indian and Alaska Native women are raped and 61 percent are assaulted in their lifetime. One some reservations, the murder rate is 10 times the national average.
- Due to exposure to violence, Native children experience rates of post-traumatic stress disorder at the same levels as Iraq and Afghanistan war veterans.

Despite these devastating rates of victimization in tribal communities, Indian tribes have largely been left out of the Crime Victims Fund (CVF), which is the federal government's principle means of providing resources for crime victims.

It is beyond debate that Alaska Native women are suffering extreme rates of domestic violence and sexual assault—rates that are disproportionately higher than that suffered by other women in the state and across the nation. There is much work that needs to be done immediately to combat this crisis, to protect Alaska Native women from violence, to increase and strengthen local life-saving services and justice to Native women survivors of this violence. Providing essential accessible resources to Indian Tribes that reach the villages in Alaska will account for successful and fair administration of crime victim funding. It is also crucial for the equitable distribution of life-saving resources to Alaska tribal governments.

Unlike state and territorial governments, who receive an annual formula distribution from the CVF, Indian tribes are only able to access CVF funds via pass-through grants from the states or by competing for very limited resources administered by the U.S. Department of Justice. According to data from the Office for Victims of Crime, in 2014, the states passed through $872,197.00—0.2 percent of available funds—to programs serving tribal victims. Of the 566 federally recognized tribes in the country, fewer than 20 received pass through grants from their respective state.

The competitive grants from USDOJ have been equally problematic. Fewer than ten tribes receive these grants each year for a three-year term, with no guarantee that this funding will be renewed. Unfortunately, without additional action by Congress, Indian tribal governments will continue to have no direct access to critical CVF funds.

Appropriate Funding is needed to provide adequate Native Village-based Services

The villages in Alaska experience high victimization rates, geographic remoteness, high poverty and cost of living, and an underdeveloped Alaska Native village-based victim services infrastructure that is the result of the historic exclusion of tribes from the CVF programs. While we know need is high, it is difficult to calculate the precise amount needed to fully meet the needs of victims in Alaska Native villages. Below are some examples of funding needs for tribal victim services and how CVF funds could be spent.

Tribal Domestic Violence and Sexual Assault Services

Native American women are assaulted at rates two and a half times the national average. Alaska Native women are disproportionately victimized at the highest rates across the country. According to the Indian Law and Order Commission report, *A Roadmap for Making Native America Safe, Chapter 2, Reforming Justice for Alaska Natives: The Time Is Now,* Alaska Native women are "over-represented in the domestic violence victim population by 250 percent; they comprise 19 percent of the population, but 47 percent of reported rape victims."

While some tribes provide services for domestic violence and sexual assault victims, resources for doing so are woefully inadequate. NEED: For FY 2014, the USDOJ's Office on Violence Against Women received applications from tribal governments requesting approximately $55.6 million for domestic violence and sexual assault services in its two primary tribal grant programs. OVW provided $33.26 million, suggesting an unmet need of at least $22 million.

Tribal Domestic Violence Shelters

There are currently fewer than 40 tribal domestic violence shelters in operation. In the State of Alaska, there is only one Native village-based Native women's shelter located in the entire state—the Emmonak Women's Shelter, which has been operating since 1979 and has been woefully underfunded. More often than not, the Emmonak Women's Shelter has not received federal or state funding and remained operational with volunteer assistance and donations. Those programs that do exist reported an unmet need of over 60,000 shelter bed nights in 2013. NEED: Building a shelter program in an additional 50 villages and tribal communities at a cost of $300,000/year would cost $15 million.

Sexual Assault Forensic Examiners

The rate of sexual violence in Indian Country, including all of Alaska's tribes far exceeds rates of sexual violence in other communities in the United States. More than two-thirds of tribal lands, however, are more than 60 minutes away from the nearest sexual assault forensic examiner. With over 229 Indian tribes represented in Alaska, the vast majority of villages are located in the remote parts of Alaska where there are no roads; access is by boat, snow machine or airplane depending on climatic conditions. For Native women in Alaska, forensic exams typically are only located in hub regions, which means she must travel by plane to a major hub that may be over 200 air miles away. NEED: To fund one trained examiner in half of the 566 tribal communities at $50,000 for salary and benefits would cost $14 million.

Services for Sex Trafficking Victims

Sex trafficking victims need specially designed services, including victim advocates to connect sexually exploited youth throughout the state with culturally appropriate support and services they need; shelters and housing; and training for criminal justice and child protective services professionals who come into contact with such victims.

According to the State of Alaska Task Force on the *Crimes of Human Trafficking, Promoting Prostitution and Sex Trafficking* 2013 report, there is "a lot of gaps in information due to the underground nature of the crime and the tendency of trafficking victims not to self-report." Although lacking in data, the Task Force acknowledges that "trafficking have occurred (and likely are occurring) in Alaska, which is why the State of Alaska has gone to great lengths to create a task force to look at the prevalence of the crimes of human trafficking and sex trafficking in Alaska; the former Governor introduced an omnibus bill addressing trafficking (which strengthened penalties for trafficking); and in 2012 the Alaska legislature amended its sex and human trafficking statutes. NEED: To fund one trafficking advocate expert in half of the 566 tribal communities at $50,000 for salary and benefits would cost $14 million.

Services for the Survivors of Homicide Victims

Services for the surviving spouses, children, and other affected family members and partners of the victims of homicides are rarely funded but sorely needed. Between 2004–2007, Alaska Natives were 2.5 times as likely to die by homicide than Alaskans who reported "White" as their race, and 2.9 times as likely to die by homicide than all Whites in the United States.

Much needed services include criminal justice advocacy, assistance in applying for victim compensation, funding to travel to trials that are out of state, legal assistance, financial counseling if the murdered victim was the sole provider, mental health counseling or other therapy, and similar services. NEED: Iowa is the rare state that has committed to supporting regional services for survivors of homicide and other violent crimes. In FY 2014, the state used $393,441 in federal grant funds to support 4 regional programs for survivors of homicide and other violent crimes. Creating 25 such programs for tribal victims would cost approximately $2.5 million.

There is Wide Support for a Creation of a Tribal Funding Stream from the CVF

Last year, NCAI, the largest national organization of American Indian and Alaska Native tribal governments, adopted Resolution ANC–14–048 urging Congress to establish a 10 percent allocation from CVF disbursements for tribes.

Recognizing the disproportionate need for victim services in tribal communities, the Office for Victims of Crime's Vision 21 report also called for increasing resources to tribal communities in order to "ensure that victims in Indian Country are no longer a footnote to this country's response to crime victims."

The USDOJ's report on American Indian and Alaska Native Children Exposed to Violence similarly called for a 10 percent tribal allocation from the CVF in its 2014 report. A 10 percent tribal allocation from the CVF has also been supported by the National Task Force to End Sexual and Domestic Violence, a coalition of more than a thousand organizations that advocate on behalf of victims of domestic violence, dating violence, sexual assault and stalking.

Conclusion

No dedicated tribal funding stream currently exists under the VOCA for Indian tribes to administer programs to compensate and provide assistance to tribal victims of crime. This lack of funding to Indian tribes is unacceptable given the extremely high rates of violence including the severity of violence committed against tribal victims of crime. The USDOJ statistics document the well-known fact that violence against Indian women is more than double that of any other population of women; yet local services are lacking or do not exist in many tribal communities and Alaska Native villages. While states and territories receive an annual formula amount from the VOCA fund, the reality is that Indian tribes do not receive such an allocation and this must be remedied immediately. We urge an amendment to VOCA to direct 10 percent of the annual disbursement from the Crime Victims Fund to tribal governments. Thank you for this opportunity and for your leadership.

_____

PREPARED STATEMENT OF JANE ROOT, EXECUTIVE DIRECTOR, WABANAKI WOMEN'S COALITION

Dear Chairman Barrasso,

Thank you for the opportunity to provide written comments regarding the Oversight Hearing on "Addressing the Needs for Victim Services in Indian Country" held on June 10, 2015. As a tribal organization that works directly with tribal victim service providers and/or tribal programs who work with victims of domestic violence, sexual assault, stalking, dating violence and other crimes, we see the devastating effects these crimes have on tribal victims and tribal communities in which they live. For victims to truly heal, it is critical that they have access to culturally appropriate crisis and recovery services, which can be made available to tribes and tribal programs under funding provided by the Crimes Victim Fund (CVF). For the following reasons described below, we ask that the unmet needs of victims on tribal lands be adequately reviewed and considered as a matter of public policy for long-term solutions and strategy that ensure that tribal victims of crimes are able to access the CVF.

A Change to VOCA Will Support Local Tribal Responses to High Crime Rates on Tribal Lands

American Indian and Alaska Natives experience the highest crime victimization rates in the country.

- American Indian and Alaska Natives are 2.5 times more likely to experience violent crime than other Americans.[1]

- Approximately 34 percent of American Indian and Alaska Native women are raped and 61 percent are assaulted in their lifetime.[2] One some reservations, the murder rate is 10 times the national average.[3]

- Approximately 1 out of 10 American Indians 12 and older become victims of violent crime annually.[4]

Despite these devastating rates of victimization in tribal communities, Indian tribes have largely been left out of the Crime Victims Fund (CVF), which is the federal government's principle means of providing resources for crime victims.

Unlike state and territorial governments, who receive an annual formula distribution from the CVF, Indian tribes are only able to access CVF funds via pass-through grants from the states or by competing for very limited resources administered by the U.S. Department of Justice. The current method of distributing federal victim services funding to tribal governments is simply not working for the Tribes in the Great Plains area where the coalition's membership serve women. According to data from the Office for Victims of Crime, in 2014, the states passed through $872,197.00—0.2 percent of available funds—to programs serving tribal victims. Of

[1] Rennison, C. (2001). Violent Victimization and Race, 1993–98. U.S. DOJ, Bureau of Justice Statistics, March, (NCJ 176354).

[2] Tjaden, P. & Thonennes. (2000). The Prevalence, Incidence, and Consequences of Violence Against Women: findings from the National Violence Survey Against Women. National Institute of Justice & the Centers for Disease Control & Prevention. _http://www.ncjrs.gov/txtfiles1/nij/183781.txt_

[3] Ronet, Bachman, et al, Violence Against American Indian and Alaska Native Women and the Criminal Justice Response: What is Known (National Institute of Justice 2007).

[4] 2004 report, American Indians and Crime, A BJS Statistical Profile, 1992–2002

the 566 federally-recognized tribes in the country, fewer than 20 received pass through grants from their respective state.

The competitive grants from USDOJ have been equally problematic. Fewer than ten tribes receive these grants each year for a three-year term, with no guarantee that this funding will be renewed. Unfortunately, without additional action by Congress, Indian tribal governments will continue to have no direct access to critical CVF funds.

Appropriate Funding Will Help Provide Adequate Native Village-based Services

Indian Tribes experience high victimization rates, geographic remoteness, high poverty and cost of living, and an underdeveloped tribally based victim services infrastructure that is the result of the historic exclusion of tribes from the CVF programs. While we know need is high, it is difficult to calculate the precise amount needed to fully meet the needs of victims on tribal lands. Below are some examples of funding needs for tribal victim services and how CVF funds could be spent.

Tribal Domestic Violence and Sexual Assault Services

Native American women are assaulted at rates two and a half times the national average. While some tribes provide services for domestic violence and sexual assault victims, resources for doing so are woefully inadequate. The USDOJ CTAS grants are highly competitive and can't begin to fund all the need for services in Indian Country.

Tribal Domestic Violence Shelters

There are currently fewer than 40 tribal domestic violence shelters in operation. Those programs that do exist reported an unmet need of over 60,000 shelter bed nights in 2013. There are two Tribal Domestic and Sexual Violence shelters in Maine but there is need for two more as the Tribes are located hours from each other.

Sexual Assault Forensic Examiners

The rate of sexual violence in Indian Country, including all of Alaska's tribes far exceeds rates of sexual violence in other communities in the United States. More than two-thirds of tribal lands, however, are more than 60 minutes away from the nearest sexual assault forensic examiner.

Services for Sex Trafficking Victims

Sex trafficking victims need specially designed services, including victim advocates to connect sexually exploited youth throughout the state with culturally appropriate support and services they need; shelters and housing; and training for criminal justice and child protective services professionals who come into contact with such victims.

Services for the Survivors of Homicide Victims

Services for the survivors of homicide victims are rarely funded but sorely needed, for surviving spouses, children, and other affected family members and partners. Much needed services include criminal justice advocacy, assistance in applying for victim compensation, funding to travel to trials that are out of state, legal assistance, financial counseling if the murdered victim was the sole provider, mental health counseling or other therapy, and similar services.

There is Wide Support for a Creation of a Tribal Funding Stream from the CVF

Last year, NCAI, the largest national organization of American Indian and Alaska Native tribal governments, adopted Resolution ANC–14–048 which supports an allocation from CVF disbursements for tribes.

Recognizing the disproportionate need for victim services in tribal communities, the Office for Victims of Crime's *Vision 21* report also called for increasing resources to tribal communities in order to "ensure that victims in Indian Country are no longer a footnote to this country's response to crime victims."[5]

The USDOJ's report on American Indian and Alaska Native Children Exposed to Violence similarly called for a tribal allocation from the CVF in its 2014 report.[6]

---

[5] Office of Justice Programs, U.S. Department of Justice, Vision 21: Transforming Victim Services Final Report, (Washington, DC: OVC, 2014).

[6] Office of Justice Programs, United States Department of Justice, Attorney General's Advisory Committee on American Indian/Alaska Native Children Exposed to Violence: Ending Violence so Children Can Thrive.

A tribal allocation from the CVF has also been supported by the National Task Force to End Sexual and Domestic Violence, a coalition of more than a thousand organizations that advocate on behalf of victims of domestic violence, dating violence, sexual assault and stalking. [7]

Conclusion

No dedicated tribal funding stream currently exists under the VOCA for Indian tribes to administer programs to compensate and provide assistance to tribal victims of crime. This lack of funding to Indian tribes is unacceptable given the extremely high rates of violence including the severity of violence committed against tribal victims of crime. The USDOJ statistics document the well-known fact that violence against Indian women is more than double that of any other population of women; yet local services are lacking or do not exist in many tribal communities and Alaska Native villages. While states and territories receive an annual formula amount from the VOCA fund, the reality is that Indian tribes do not receive such an allocation and this must be remedied immediately. We request a policy shift that will provide for, through an amendment to VOCA, an annual disbursement from the Crime Victims Fund to tribal governments. Thank you for this opportunity to present a summary of recent findings on this issue and for your leadership.

PREPARED STATEMENT OF GERMAINE OMISH-GUACHENA, EXECUTIVE DIRECTOR, STRONG HEARTED NATIVE WOMEN'S COALITION, INC.

Dear Chairman Barrasso,

Thank you for the opportunity to provide written comments regarding the Oversight Hearing on ''Addressing the Needs for Victim Services in Indian Country'' held on June 10, 2015. As a tribal organization that works directly with tribal victim service providers and/or tribal programs who work with victims of domestic violence, sexual assault, stalking, dating violence and other crimes, we see the devastating effects these crimes have on tribal victims and tribal communities in which they live. For victims to truly heal, it is critical that they have access to culturally appropriate crisis and recovery services, which can be made available to tribes and tribal programs under funding provided by the Crimes Victim Fund (CVF). For the following reasons described below, we ask that the unmet needs of victims on tribal lands be adequately reviewed and considered as a matter of public policy for long-term solutions and strategy that ensure that tribal victims of crimes are able to access the CVF.

A Change to VOCA Will Support Local Tribal Responses to High Crime Rates on Tribal Lands

American Indian and Alaska Natives experience the highest crime victimization rates in the country.

- American Indian and Alaska Natives are 2.5 times more likely to experience violent crime than other Americans. [1]

- Approximately 34 percent of American Indian and Alaska Native women are raped and 61 percent are assaulted in their lifetime. [2] One some reservations, the murder rate is 10 times the national average. [3]

- Approximately 1 out of 10 American Indians 12 and older become victims of violent crime annually. [4]

---

[7] NTF Letter to Appropriators, April 15, 2015, available at *http://4vawa.org/4vawa/2015/4/21/ntf-urges-for-increase-funding-for-federal-programs-that-address-domestic-violence-sexual-assault-dating-violence-and-stalking.*

[1] Rennison, C. (2001). Violent Victimization and Race, 1993–98. U.S. DOJ, Bureau of Justice Statistics, March, (NCJ 176354).

[2] Tjaden, P. & Thonennes. (2000). The Prevalence, Incidence, and Consequences of Violence Against Women: findings from the National Violence Survey Against Women. National Institute of Justice & the Centers for Disease Control & Prevention. *http://www.ncjrs.gov/txtfiles1/nij/183781.txt*

[3] Ronet, Bachman, et al, Violence Against American Indian and Alaska Native Women and the Criminal Justice Response: What is Known (National Institute of Justice 2007).

[4] 2004 report, American Indians and Crime, A BJS Statistical Profile, 1992–2002

Despite these devastating rates of victimization in tribal communities, Indian tribes have largely been left out of the Crime Victims Fund (CVF), which is the federal government's principle means of providing resources for crime victims.

Unlike state and territorial governments, who receive an annual formula distribution from the CVF, Indian tribes are only able to access CVF funds via pass-through grants from the states or by competing for very limited resources administered by the U.S. Department of Justice. The current method of distributing federal victim services funding to tribal governments is simply not working for the Tribes in the Great Plains area where the coalition's membership serve women. According to data from the Office for Victims of Crime, in 2014, the states passed through $872,197.00—0.2 percent of available funds—to programs serving tribal victims. Of the 566 federally-recognized tribes in the country, fewer than 20 received pass through grants from their respective state.

The competitive grants from USDOJ have been equally problematic. Fewer than ten tribes receive these grants each year for a three-year term, with no guarantee that this funding will be renewed. Unfortunately, without additional action by Congress, Indian tribal governments will continue to have no direct access to critical CVF funds.

Appropriate Funding Will Help Provide Adequate Native Village-based Services

Tribal communities have sovereignty to establish tribal laws, however, California is a PL280state that requires state court participation. This Act transferred federal criminal jurisdiction tothe State of California without any resources to support the increased responsibility ofresponding to crimes occurring upon Indian lands. The impact upon the lives of Native womenon Indian reservations is the lack of adequate criminal and civil justice and culturally sensitiveservices to protect women. Often local and tribal law enforcement personnel are themselves notfamiliar with the myriad of jurisdictional issues, especially in relation to people living on theIndian reservations. As a result, many service professionals are confused or unsure of the uniquebarriers and challenges victims face when attempting to break free from a violent perpetrator.

Strong Hearted Native Women's Coalition, Inc. was founded in 2005 to bring awareness againstSexual Assault, Domestic Violence, Youth Violence, and Stalking in North County of the SanDiego County. Native women from the Indian reservations of Rincon, Pauma, Mesa Grande,Santa Ysabel, La Jolla, San Pasqual, Los Coyotes, Pala, and Inaja/Cosmit make-up our coalitionmembership. Over the years, our coalition has expanded to include tribes from all of SouthernCalifornia as well as other tribes throughout the state of California.

Our coalition is a member organization of a newly formed national organization, the Alliance ofTribal Coalitions to End Violence, (ATCEV), which consists of all the OVW tribal coalitionsthroughout the country, allowing for a national resource. We are working in our communities toassist in the essential change needed to reduce Sexual Assault, Domestic Violence, YouthViolence, Human Trafficking, and Stalking to Native American women, their families, and theircommunity.

Indian Tribes experience high victimization rates, geographic remoteness, high poverty and costof living, and an underdeveloped tribally based victim services infrastructure that is the result ofthe historic exclusion of tribes from the CVF programs. While we know need is high, it isdifficult to calculate the precise amount needed to fully meet the needs of victims on tribal lands.Below are some examples of funding needs for tribal victim services and how CVF funds couldbe spent.

Tribal Domestic Violence and Sexual Assault Services

Native American women are assaulted at rates two and a half times the national average. While some tribes provide services for domestic violence and sexual assault victims, resources for doing so are woefully inadequate.

Tribal Domestic Violence Shelters

There are currently fewer than 40 tribal domestic violence shelters in operation. Those programs that do exist reported an unmet need of over 60,000 shelter bed nights in 2013. Our coalition recently open our shelter doors in September of 2014 and has been full the whole time. We struggle to meet the needs of all our "guests" in our Kiicha House. We rely on very limited funding.

Sexual Assault Forensic Examiners

The rate of sexual violence in Indian Country, including all of Alaska's tribes far exceeds rates of sexual violence in other communities in the United States. More than two-thirds of tribal lands, however, are more than 60 minutes away from the nearest sexual assault forensic examiner. Our coalition has been working with two

Tribal SART working groups and we have been attempting to work with our local San Diego County Sheriff's Department and the San Diego District Attorney's office to work on a way to make this happen. We have the facilities and the equipment through both Indian Health Services facilities in San Diego County. Both the San Diego County Sheriff's Department and the San Diego District Attorney's office have given the working groups opposition in assisting us. This endeavor would give the County of San Diego two more SANE facilities in the county and would be located on the two reservations where the Indian Health facilities are located, which brings the SANE facility closer to our Native communities.

Services for Sex Trafficking Victims

Sex trafficking victims need specially designed services, including victim advocates to connect sexually exploited youth throughout the state with culturally appropriate support and services they need; shelters and housing; and training for criminal justice and child protective services professionals who come into contact with such victims.

Services for the Survivors of Homicide Victims

Services for the survivors of homicide victims are rarely funded but sorely needed, for surviving spouses, children, and other affected family members and partners. Much needed services include criminal justice advocacy, assistance in applying for victim compensation, funding to travel to trials that are out of state, legal assistance, financial counseling if the murdered victim was the sole provider, mental health counseling or other therapy, and similar services.

There is Wide Support for a Creation of a Tribal Funding Stream from the CVF

Last year, NCAI, the largest national organization of American Indian and Alaska Native tribal governments, adopted Resolution ANC–14–048 which supports an allocation from CVF disbursements for tribes.

Recognizing the disproportionate need for victim services in tribal communities, the Office for Victims of Crime's *Vision 21* report also called for increasing resources to tribal communities in order to "ensure that victims in Indian Country are no longer a footnote to this country's response to crime victims."[5]

The USDOJ's report on American Indian and Alaska Native Children Exposed to Violence similarly called for a tribal allocation from the CVF in its 2014 report.[6]

A tribal allocation from the CVF has also been supported by the National Task Force to End Sexual and Domestic Violence, a coalition of more than a thousand organizations that advocate on behalf of victims of domestic violence, dating violence, sexual assault and stalking.[7]

Law enforcement response to these shocking rates of domestic and sexual violence can be crucial to providing safety, resources, and protection for survivors and their families. An important foundation for an appropriate response by law enforcement is for peace offices to have a clear understand of PL 280 and its implications for their work in these communities. AB 373 (Medina) would have helped to ensure that officers who may be responding to calls for service on tribal lands have the information they need about PL 280. AB 373, would have required peace officers employed by the agency who work in, or adjacent to, Indian tribal lands, or who may be responsible for responding to calls for service on, or adjacent to, Indian tribal lands, to receive training on Public Law 280 (PL 280). We believe this is a common-sense requirement that will help increase safety for tribal victims and enhance law enforcement's response to these calls for service. In 2015 our coalition helped to support Assembly Bill 373 (Medina), which did not pass because law enforcement does not want to pay for it and so they opposed this bill.

Conclusion

No dedicated tribal funding stream currently exists under the VOCA for Indian tribes to administer programs to compensate and provide assistance to tribal victims of crime. This lack of funding to Indian tribes is unacceptable given the extremely high rates of violence including the severity of violence committed against tribal vic-

[5] Office of Justice Programs, U.S. Department of Justice, Vision 21: Transforming Victim Services Final Report, (Washington, DC: OVC, 2014).

[6] Office of Justice Programs, United States Department of Justice, Attorney General's Advisory Committee on American Indian/Alaska Native Children Exposed to Violence: Ending Violence so Children Can Thrive.

[7] NTF Letter to Appropriators, April 15, 2015, available at *http://4vawa.org/4vawa/2015/4/21/ntf-urges-for-increase-funding-for-federal-programs-that-address-domestic-violence-sexual-assault-dating-violence-and-stalking.*

tims of crime. The USDOJ statistics document the well-known fact that violence against Indian women is more than double that of any other population of women; yet local services are lacking or do not exist in many tribal communities and Alaska Native villages. While states and territories receive an annual formula amount from the VOCA fund, the reality is that Indian tribes do not receive such an allocation and this must be remedied immediately. We request a policy shift that will provide for, through an amendment to VOCA, an annual disbursement from the Crime Victims Fund to tribal governments. Thank you for this opportunity to present a summary of recent findings on this issue and for your leadership.

———

PREPARED STATEMENT OF THE NATIONAL CONGRESS OF AMERICAN INDIANS (NCAI)

On behalf of the National Congress of American Indians (NCAI), we are pleased to present testimony to the Senate Committee on Indian Affairs on "Addressing the Need for Victim Services in Indian Country." American Indians and Alaska Natives experience the highest crime victimization rates in the country. When crime occurs, victims and survivors have a variety of needs that may include mental health counseling, appropriate medical care, support during criminal justice proceedings, and emergency financial and housing assistance. Complex jurisdictional issues, along with the cultural diversity of tribes and the basic reality of geography, pose a significant challenge for crime victims in need of services in Indian Country. Since the passage of the Victims of Crime Act (VOCA) in 1984, the federal government has provided significant support to crime victim services programs across the country. As is unfortunately too often the case, Indian Country has largely been left out of this effort. Crime victims on tribal lands still struggle to access even the most basic services. As the Committee considers this important issue, we urge you to support amendments to VOCA that would appropriately recognize the important role tribal governments play in providing services to crime victims in their communities.

Crime Victims Fund

Since its creation in 1984 through VOCA, the Crime Victims Fund (CVF) has been the federal government's primary funding source for supporting crime victim compensation and assistance. Each year millions of dollars are deposited into the fund from the penalties assessed against convicted criminals. The CVF was founded on the basic premise that money from federal criminals should be used to help crime victims. The VOCA statute allocates funds made available from the CVF for a host of purposes, including a small discretionary tribal grant program through the Children's Justice Act to improve the investigation and prosecution of child abuse cases in tribal communities. There is generally about $2.7 million available for 566 Indian tribes each year in this program. The bulk of CVF funds are distributed to state and territorial governments as a formula grant, which they then sub-grant to victim assistance programs in their jurisdiction. Tribal governments, however, do not receive a similar formula distribution from the CVF. Other than the tribal CJA program, Indian tribes are able to access CVF funds for victim services only via sub-grants from the states, or by competing for very limited resources that the Department of Justice chooses to make available from its discretionary allocation. Both of these mechanisms have failed to provide adequate funding for tribal victim services programs.

NCAI recently submitted a request to the Office for Victims of Crime (OVC) under the Freedom of Information Act asking for information about sub-grants made by states to programs serving American Indian and Alaska Native victims over the past five years. NCAI received the attached spreadsheets in response, * which show that pass-through funding has proven wholly unsuccessful in distributing funds to tribal victim service providers. According to data from OVC, from 2010–2014, the states passed through 0.5 percent of available funds to programs serving tribal victims, less than $2.5 million annually. New Mexico, where American Indians make up 10.7 percent of the population, subgranted less than 1 percent of total available funds to programs serving Indian victims during that time period. Oklahoma, a state that is frequently held up as a place where the VOCA sub-grant process is working and where the Indian population is 12.9 percent, has never sub-granted more than 5.5 percent of its funds to programs serving Indians victims. And in Alaska, where Alaska Natives make up 19.4 percent of the population, the state of Alaska reports that from 2010–2013 it sub-granted between 0 and 3.9 percent of funds received through VOCA to programs serving Native victims. The vast majority of

---

* The information referred to has been retained in the Committee files.

existing tribal victim service programs we have spoken to report that they are not able to access these funds at all.

Given that pass-through funding is not reaching tribal victims, tribal governments must largely rely upon the discretionary grant funding made available by OVC. OVC originally established a Victim Assistance in Indian Country (VAIC) discretionary grant program in 1989 in response to revelations about multiple victim molestations perpetrated by Bureau of Indian Affairs teachers in several reservation communities. [1] In attempting to identify services for the child victims, OVC realized that "funding to on reservation victim assistance programs was virtually non-existent." [2] VAIC funding was awarded for a three year period to state applicants who had partnered with tribal programs. OVC hoped that structuring the grant program to require state-tribal collaboration would help integrate tribal programs into the state VOCA programs and that the states would continue to fund the tribal programs after the federal grant ended. The states did not continue funding tribal programs at the conclusion of the three-year grant, however, and in 1998 OVC discontinued the failed pass-through model and began funding tribal programs directly. [3] Today this program is known as the Comprehensive Tribal Victim Assistance Program (TVAP).

While the TVAP is an improvement over the pass-through model used previously, its success is hampered by the low level of funding available and the short-term discretionary nature of the grants. Approximately $3 million has been available annually through this program in recent years. Tribes must compete against one another to access these funds, and fewer than 10 tribes receive these grants each year for a three-year term, with no guarantee that this funding will be renewed. [4] Too often when a grant ends, tribal programs must completely shut down. As the Committee considers this critical issue, our foremost request is that tribal victims services are not set up as another short-term grant program. Tribal governments need sustainable funding to meet the needs of victims into the foreseeable future, not a short-term program at risk of disappearing soon after it is fully established.

Last year, NCAI adopted Resolution ANC–14–048 (attached) urging Congress to create an "above-the-cap" reserve in the Victims of Crime Act for tribal governments, or alternatively, to establish a 10 percent allocation from CVF disbursements for tribal governments. The Attorney General's Task Force on American Indian and Alaska Native Children Exposed to Violence similarly called for a 10 percent tribal allocation from the CVF in its 2014 report. [5] A 10 percent tribal allocation from the CVF has also been supported by the National Task Force to End Sexual and Domestic Violence, a coalition of more than a thousand organizations that advocate on behalf of victims of domestic violence, dating violence, sexual assault and stalking. [6] OVC has also recognized the disproportionate need for victim services in tribal communities. Its Vision 21 report singled out tribal communities and called for increasing resources in order to "ensure that victims in Indian Country are no longer a footnote to this country's response to crime victims." [7]

In recent years, annual disbursements from the CVF have been about $700 million. Collections, however, reached as high as $2.8 billion in 2013, leaving a balance in the fund of more than $13 billion. There has been significant pressure on Congress to make this money available for crime victims, and Congress significantly increased the disbursements from the CVF for FY 2015 to $2.3 billion. Despite this three-fold increase, none of the money was directed to Indian tribes. There is language in the FY 2016 Budget Resolution that will likely result in even higher disbursements this year. Without additional action by Congress, however, Indian tribal

---

[1] CCAN, "History of Federal Victim Assistance Services and Programs in Indian Country," Upon the Back of a Turtle, (1998), *available at http://www.icctc.org/B-Ch%204%20victim%20asst%20svcs.pdf*

[2] *Id.*

[3] *Id.*

[4] OVC reports that with the significant increase in disbursements from the Crime Victims Fund for FY 2015 they will be funding 24 tribal programs for FY 2015, instead of the usual 8 programs. We anticipate that total funding will be about $10 million.

[5] Office of Justice Programs, United States Department of Justice, Attorney General's Advisory Committee on American Indian/Alaska Native Children Exposed to Violence: Ending Violence so Children Can Thrive, (Washington, D.C.: OJJOP, November 2014) (http://www.washingtonpost.com/r/2010–2019/WashingtonPost/2014/11/17/Nati. . ., accessed June 8, 2015).

[6] NTF Letter to Appropriators, April 15, 2015, *available at http://4vawa.org/4vawa/2015/4/21/ntf-urges-for-increasefunding-for-federal-programs-that-address-domestic-violence-sexual-assault-dating-violence-and-stalking.*

[7] Office of Justice Programs, U.S. Department of Justice, *Vision 21: Transforming Victim Services Final Report,* (Washington, DC: OVC, 2014).

governments will continue to have no direct access to critical CVF funds, and victims in Indian Country will once again be left behind.

Need for Victims Services

American Indians and Alaska Natives experience the highest rates of violent victimization in the country. The rate of aggravated assault among American Indians and Alaska Natives is roughly twice that of the country as a whole (600.2 per 100,000 versus 323.6 per 100,000).[8] The Bureau of Justice Statistics has estimated that 1 out of 10 American Indians 12 and older become victims of violent crime annually.[9] At the same time, the historic lack of funding for tribal victims services programs means that the infrastructure for providing victims services in tribal communities is woefully underdeveloped. The services that are available are provided by a complicated and fragmented system that includes federal, state, tribal, and private actors. Programs struggle to find stable sources of funding and often close when grant funds run out. There is no comprehensive compilation of the services that are available in Indian Country, nor a comprehensive analysis of the gaps. The information that is available, however, makes clear that many of the most vulnerable Native victims do not have access to the services they need.

Child Advocacy Centers

Children's Advocacy Centers (CACs), for example, are a recognized best practice for providing a child-focused, multidisciplinary response to child abuse, especially child sexual abuse. Children who receive services at CACs are twice as likely to receive specialized medical exams and significantly more likely to receive referrals for specialized mental health treatment.[10] American Indian and Alaska Native children are 50 percent more likely to experience child abuse and sexual abuse than white children.[11] Due to exposure to violence, Native children experience post-traumatic stress disorder at a rate of 22 percent—the same levels as Iraq and Afghanistan war veterans and triple the rate of the rest of the population.[12]

Despite the increased victimization risk for Native American children, very few CACs exist on tribal lands. While some tribal communities may be served by CACs off the reservation, the average driving distance to a CAC from tribal lands is 62 miles. For more than 100 tribal communities, the driving distance is between 100 and 300 miles.[13] For example, a child abuse victim on the Rosebud Reservation in South Dakota must travel two and a half hours across the state (or more in bad weather) to reach a CAC.[14] Even where tribal CACs exist, tribes struggle to find stable funding to maintain the programs. For example, the Eastern Shoshone Tribe opened a CAC on the Wind River Reservation in 2013 after an existing CAC operated by the Northern Arapaho Tribe ran out of funding and closed.[15] The new CAC is dependent on a three-year federal grant with no guarantee that funding will be renewed after the grant period ends.

Domestic Violence Shelters

Nearly 61 percent of Native women are assaulted during their lifetime. One local study found that 1 in 12 Native women experience violence perpetrated by their

---

[8] Rennison, C. (2001). Violent Victimization and Race, 1993–98. U.S. DOJ, Bureau of Justice Statistics, March, (NCJ176354).

[9] 2004 report, American Indians and Crime, A BJS Statistical Profile, 1992–2002

[10] Randall Cooper, ''Children's Advocacy Centers and Indian Country,'' Update: National Center for Prosecution of Child Abuse, vol. 24, no 2 (2014), *available at http://www.ndaa.org/pdf/Update%20Vol24lNo2.pdf.*

[11] Children's Bureau, U.S. Department of Health and Human Services, Child Maltreatment 2011, 28 (2012). Rates of child maltreatment in certain states are even more alarming. According to data from the Department of Health & Human Services, Native children in Alaska experience maltreatment at a rate more than six and a half times the rate for white children. In North Dakota, the rate of maltreatment for Native children is more than three times the rate for white children.

[12] Attorney General's Advisory Committee on American Indian/Alaska Native Children Exposed to Violence, supra note 3, at 38.

[13] Randall Cooper, ''Children's Advocacy Centers and Indian Country,'' Update: National Center for Prosecution of Child Abuse, vol. 24, no 2 (2014), *available at http://www.ndaa.org/pdf/Update%20Vol24lNo2.pdf*

[14] *Id.*

[15] Rebecca Martinez, ''Child Advocacy Center Opens on Wind River Reservation,'' Wyoming Public Media, January 24, 2013, *available at http://wyomingpublicmedia.org/post/child-advocacy-center-opens-wind-river-reservation.*

husband every year.[16] On some reservations, the murder rate of Native women is 10 times the national average.[17] Domestic violence shelters provide essential services to victims of domestic violence. In addition to emergency housing for a woman and her children fleeing abuse, they often provide counseling, advocacy, legal services, and referrals to other services. There are currently fewer than 40 tribal domestic violence shelters in operation. Those programs that do exist struggle to find sufficient funding to maintain their operations. The domestic violence shelter on the Pine Ridge reservation, for example, closed 8 years ago. Advocates report that in order to access shelter, they must transfer victims-and often their children-at least 100 miles one way to a shelter in Rapid City. When shelter space is not available in Rapid City, advocates drive victims 700 miles to Sioux Falls.[18]

The Emmonak Women's Shelter, the only domestic violence shelter located in an Alaska Native village, has faced similar challenges. Like so many victim services programs in Indian Country, the shelter is reliant on short-term, discretionary funding from the federal government in order to remain operational. This two-bedroom shelter serves 500 women a year from 13 surrounding Native communities. Given the geographic isolation of the region, it is generally the only option for local women seeking to escape abuse. In operation since 1978, the shelter was forced to temporarily close in 2005 after the state of Alaska eliminated funding for this and a number of other rural services for Alaska Natives. Even while closed, battered women sought refuge there. Met with locked doors, women climbed surrounding trees and even hid in trash cans to escape their abusers. The shelter was able to reopen months later after securing funding from a tribal non-profit, and months after that, it received its first federal grant.[19] The shelter temporarily closed again in 2012 after running out of its DOJ funding due to high fuel costs during an especially brutal winter. The shelter was able to reopen after obtaining $30,000 in private donations and a $50,000 emergency grant from the Bureau of Indian Affairs. Staff took pay cuts and rationed fuel in order to conserve the little funding they had.[20]

Sexual Assault Forensic Examiners and Sexual Assault Response Teams

Access to services for sexual assault survivors is similarly limited. Approximately 34 percent of Native women are raped in their lifetime, and nearly half will experience sexual violence other than rape within their lifetime.[21] When Native women are raped, they are more likely to experience other physical violence during the attack, their attacker is more likely to have a weapon, and they are more likely to have injuries requiring medical attention.[22]

Sexual Assault Examiner (SAE) and Sexual Assault Response Team (SART) programs have been shown to improve both the care of survivors of sexual assault and criminal justice outcomes in sexual assault cases.[23] SAEs and SARTs are instrumental in facilitating immediate access to appropriate health care and other services for victims and for minimizing re-victimization by the justice system. A 2014 study used GIS mapping to evaluate proximity of trained forensic examiners to 650 census-identified Native American lands. The study found that more than two-thirds of Native American lands are more than 60 minutes away from the nearest sexual assault forensic examiner.[24]

Conclusion

We expect that disbursements from the CVF this year may well exceed $2.5 billion. Particularly at a time when funding is significantly increasing, it would be un-

---

[16]R. Bachman, et al, ''Violence Against American Indian and Alaska Native Women and the Criminal Justice Response: What is Known,'' (2008), *available at https://www.ncjrs.gov/pdffiles1/nij/grants/223691.pdf.*

[17]R. Bachman, et al, ''Violence Against American Indian and Alaska Native Women and the Criminal Justice Response: What is Known,'' (2008), *available at https://www.ncjrs.gov/pdffiles1/nij/grants/223691.pdf.*

[18]Conversation with advocates from the Pine Ridge reservation on June 2, 2015 at the Women Are Sacred conference.

[19]Timothy Williams, In Remote Alaska, Financing Puts a Rare Refuge at Risk, N.Y. TIMES, May 23, 2012, at A3.

[20]Timothy Williams, With Grant, an Alaska Women's Shelter, N.Y. TIMES, July 6, 2012, at A15.

[21]*The National Intimate Partner and Sexual Violence Survey (NISVS): 2010 summary report,* Atlanta, GA: National Center for Injury Prevention and Control, Centers for Disease Control and Prevention (2011).

[22]R. Bachman, et al, ''Violence Against American Indian and Alaska Native Women and the Criminal Justice Response: What is Known,'' (2008), p. 36, *available at https://www.ncjrs.gov/pdffiles1/nij/grants/223691.pdf.*

[23]Jennifer Giroux, Ashley Juraska, Eric Wood & Lindsey Wood, *Sexual Assault Services coverage on Native American Land,* 10 Journal of Forensic Nursing, 92, 92 (2014).

[24]*Id.*

conscionable to continue to ignore the needs of the most victimized population in the United States. Now is the time to make sure that crime victims in tribal communities have access to the crime victim assistance and compensation that they desperately need. Creating a dedicated tribal funding allocation from the CVF would provide a stable source of funding for Indian tribes to develop the victims services infrastructure that is taken for granted in much of the rest of the country. We look forward to continuing to work with the Committee to address this issue.

Attachment

THE NATIONAL CONGRESS OF AMERICAN INDIANS—RESOLUTION #ANC–14–048

TITLE: Support for a dedicated Tribal Set-Aside in the Victims of Crime Act (VOCA) Fund

WHEREAS, we, the members of the National Congress of American Indians of the United States, invoking the divine blessing of the Creator upon our efforts and purposes, in order to preserve for ourselves and our descendants the inherent sovereign rights of our Indian nations, rights secured under Indian treaties and agreements with the United States, and all other rights and benefits to which we are entitled under the laws and Constitution of the United States, to enlighten the public toward a better understanding of the Indian people, to preserve Indian cultural values, and otherwise promote the health, safety and welfare of the Indian people, do hereby establish and submit the following resolution; and

WHEREAS, the National Congress of American Indians (NCAI) was established in 1944 and is the oldest and largest national organization of American Indian and Alaska Native tribal governments; and

WHEREAS, the Crime Victims Fund, administered by the Office for Victims of Crime (OVC) within DOJ's Office of Justice Programs (OJP), was initially established to address the need for victim services programs, and to assist tribal, state, and local governments in providing appropriate services to their communities; and

WHEREAS, Congress passed the Victims of Crimes Act thirty years ago and did not include Indian tribes in the original distribution of funds; and

WHEREAS, the Fund is financed by collections of fines, penalty assessments, and bond forfeitures from defendants convicted of Federal crimes, but until now, tribes have only been eligible to receive a very small portion of the discretionary funding from the Fund; and

WHEREAS, in FY 2000, Congress began limiting the amount of Fund deposits that could be obligated each year. This was to provide a stable level of funding available for these programs in future years despite annual fluctuations in Fund deposits; and

WHEREAS, in $2.8 billion and as a result the Fund now holds balances in excess of $10 billion enough under the current spending cap to last 12 years; and

WHEREAS, OVC and OJP officials have recognized the great need to strengthen victims services on tribal lands and, thus, are proposing this new set-aside to help meet that need; and

WHEREAS, the new tribal funding is requested as part of OVC's Vision 21 Initiative, a strategic planning initiative based on an 18-month national assessment by OJP that systematically engaged the crime victim advocacy field and other stakeholder groups in assessing current and emerging challenges and opportunities facing the field; and

WHEREAS, Indian nations and tribal service providers require essential resources to respond to violence perpetrated against American Indian and Alaska Native women, as well as to provide services to women victims seeking assistance.

NOW THEREFORE BE IT RESOLVED, that the NCAI does hereby support the increase in the amount of money released from the Crime Victim's Fund to include a dedicated funding stream for Indian tribes to meet the dire needs of tribal victims; and

BE IT FURTHER RESOLVED, that the NCAI does hereby support the creation of an "above the cap" reserve in the Victims of Crime Act (VOCA), or alternatively, a 10 percent VOCA tribal set-aside, that would fund tribes and tribal government programs and non-profit, non-governmental tribal organizations, located within the jurisdictional boundaries of an Indian reservation, Alaska Native Villages, and Indian areas that provide services to Native women victimized by domestic and/or sexual violence; and

BE IT FINALLY RESOLVED, that this resolution shall be the policy of NCAI until it is withdrawn or modified by subsequent resolution.

CERTIFICATION

The foregoing resolution was adopted by the General Assembly at the 2014 Mid-Year Session of the National Congress of American Indians, held at the Dena'ina Civic & Convention Center, June 8–11, 2014 in Anchorage, Alaska, with a quorum present.

PREPARED STATEMENT OF HON. CASIMERO ACEVEDA JR. PRESIDENT, ORGANIZED VILLAGE OF KAKE

Dear Chairman Barrasso,

Thank you for the opportunity to provide written comments regarding the Oversight Hearing on "Addressing the Needs for Victim Services in Indian Country" held on June 10, 2015. The Organized Village of Kake respectfully requests that 42 U.S.C. 10602 (b) be amended to include, "Federally recognized Indian tribes" as eligible for the Victim Crimes Compensation fund. It is further our request that a minimum of 10 percent of authorized funds be Congressionally appropriated to American Indian and Alaska Native Tribal governments for the reasons described below.

A Change to VOCA is needed to Support Local Tribal Responses to High Crime Rates on Tribal Lands as Recommended by the Indian Law & Order Commission Report, "A Roadmap for Making Native America Safer"

American Indian and Alaska Natives experience the highest crime victimization rates in the country.

- American Indian and Alaska Natives are 2.5 times more likely to experience violent crime than other Americans.
- Approximately 34 percent of American Indian and Alaska Native women are raped and 61 percent are assaulted in their lifetime. One some reservations, the murder rate is 10 times the national average.
- Due to exposure to violence, Native children experience rates of post-traumatic stress disorder at the same levels as Iraq and Afghanistan war veterans.

Despite these devastating rates of victimization in tribal communities, Indian tribes have largely been left out of the Crime Victims Fund (CVF), which is the federal government's principle means of providing resources for crime victims.

It is beyond debate that Alaska Native women are suffering extreme rates of domestic violence and sexual assault—rates that are disproportionately higher than that suffered by other women in the state and across the nation. There is much work that needs to be done immediately to combat this crisis, to protect Alaska Native women from violence, to increase and strengthen local life-saving services and justice to Native women survivors of this violence. Providing essential accessible resources to Indian Tribes that reach the villages in Alaska will account for successful and fair administration of crime victim funding. It is also crucial for the equitable distribution of life-saving resources to Alaska tribal governments.

Unlike state and territorial governments, who receive an annual formula distribution from the CVF, Indian tribes are only able to access CVF funds via pass-through grants from the states or by competing for very limited resources administered by the U.S. Department of Justice. According to data from the Office for Victims of Crime, in 2014, the states passed through $872,197.00—0.2 percent of available funds—to programs serving tribal victims. Of the 566 federally recognized tribes in the country, fewer than 20 received pass through grants from their respective state.

The competitive grants from USDOJ have been equally problematic. Fewer than ten tribes receive these grants each year for a three-year term, with no guarantee that this funding will be renewed. Unfortunately, without additional action by Congress, Indian tribal governments will continue to have no direct access to critical CVF funds.

Appropriate Funding is needed to provide adequate Native Village-based Services

The villages in Alaska experience high victimization rates, geographic remoteness, high poverty and cost of living, and an underdeveloped Alaska Native village-based victim services infrastructure that is the result of the historic exclusion of tribes from the CVF programs. While we know need is high, it is difficult to calculate the precise amount needed to fully meet the needs of victims in Alaska Native villages. Below are some examples of funding needs for tribal victim services and how CVF funds could be spent.

Tribal Domestic Violence and Sexual Assault Services

Native American women are assaulted at rates two and a half times the national average. Alaska Native women are disproportionately victimized at the highest rates across the country. According to the Indian Law and Order Commission report, *A Roadmap for Making Native America Safe,* Chapter 2, *Reforming Justice for Alaska Natives: The Time Is Now,* Alaska Native women are "over-represented in the domestic violence victim population by 250 percent; they comprise 19 percent of the population, but 47 percent of reported rape victims."

While some tribes provide services for domestic violence and sexual assault victims, resources for doing so are woefully inadequate. NEED: For FY 2014, the USDOJ's Office on Violence Against Women received applications from tribal governments requesting approximately $55.6 million for domestic violence and sexual assault services in its two primary tribal grant programs. OVW provided $33.26 million, suggesting an unmet need of at least $22 million.

Tribal Domestic Violence Shelters

There are currently fewer than 40 tribal domestic violence shelters in operation. In the State of Alaska, there is only one Native village-based Native women's shelter located in the entire state—the Emmonak Women's Shelter, which has been operating since 1979 and has been woefully underfunded. More often than not, the Emmonak Women's Shelter has not received federal or state funding and remained operational with volunteer assistance and donations. Those programs that do exist reported an unmet need of over 60,000 shelter bed nights in 2013. NEED: Building a shelter program in an additional 50 villages and tribal communities at a cost of $300,000/year would cost $15 million.

Sexual Assault Forensic Examiners

The rate of sexual violence in Indian Country, including all of Alaska's tribes far exceeds rates of sexual violence in other communities in the United States. More than two-thirds of tribal lands, however, are more than 60 minutes away from the nearest sexual assault forensic examiner. With over 229 Indian tribes represented in Alaska, the vast majority of villages are located in the remote parts of Alaska where there are no roads; access is by boat, snow machine or airplane depending on climatic conditions. For Native women in Alaska, forensic exams typically are only located in hub regions, which means she must travel by plane to a major hub that may be over 200 air miles away. NEED: To fund one trained examiner in half of the 566 tribal communities at $50,000 for salary and benefits would cost $14 million.

Services for Sex Trafficking Victims

Sex trafficking victims need specially designed services, including victim advocates to connect sexually exploited youth throughout the state with culturally appropriate support and services they need; shelters and housing; and training for criminal justice and child protective services professionals who come into contact with such victims.

According to the State of Alaska Task Force on the *Crimes of Human Trafficking, Promoting Prostitution and Sex Trafficking* 2013 report, there is "a lot of gaps in information due to the underground nature of the crime and the tendency of trafficking victims not to self-report." Although lacking in data, the Task Force acknowledges that "trafficking have occurred (and likely are occurring) in Alaska, which is why the State of Alaska has gone to great lengths to create a task force to look at the prevalence of the crimes of human trafficking and sex trafficking in Alaska; the former Governor introduced an omnibus bill addressing trafficking (which strengthened penalties for trafficking); and in 2012 the Alaska legislature amended its sex and human trafficking statutes. NEED: To fund one trafficking advocate expert in half of the 566 tribal communities at $50,000 for salary and benefits would cost $14 million.

Services for the Survivors of Homicide Victims

Services for the surviving spouses, children, and other affected family members and partners of the victims of homicides are rarely funded but sorely needed. Between 2004–2007, Alaska Natives were 2.5 times as likely to die by homicide than Alaskans who reported "White" as their race, and 2.9 times as likely to die by homicide than all Whites in the United States.

Much needed services include criminal justice advocacy, assistance in applying for victim compensation, funding to travel to trials that are out of state, legal assistance, financial counseling if the murdered victim was the sole provider, mental health counseling or other therapy, and similar services. NEED: Iowa is the rare state that has committed to supporting regional services for survivors of homicide and other violent crimes. In FY 2014, the state used $393,441 in federal grant funds to support 4 regional programs for survivors of homicide and other violent crimes. Creating 25 such programs for tribal victims would cost approximately $2.5 million.

There is Wide Support for a Creation of a Tribal Funding Stream from the CVF

Last year, NCAI, the largest national organization of American Indian and Alaska Native tribal governments, adopted Resolution ANC–14–048 urging Congress to establish a 10 percent allocation from CVF disbursements for tribes.

Recognizing the disproportionate need for victim services in tribal communities, the Office for Victims of Crime's *Vision 21* report also called for increasing resources to tribal communities in order to "ensure that victims in Indian Country are no longer a footnote to this country's response to crime victims."

The USDOJ's report on American Indian and Alaska Native Children Exposed to Violence similarly called for a 10 percent tribal allocation from the CVF in its 2014 report. A 10 percent tribal allocation from the CVF has also been supported by the National Task Force to End Sexual and Domestic Violence, a coalition of more than a thousand organizations that advocate on behalf of victims of domestic violence, dating violence, sexual assault and stalking.

Conclusion

No dedicated tribal funding stream currently exists under the VOCA for Indian tribes to administer programs to compensate and provide assistance to tribal victims of crime. This lack of funding to Indian tribes is unacceptable given the extremely high rates of violence including the severity of violence committed against tribal victims of crime. The USDOJ statistics document the well-known fact that violence against Indian women is more than double that of any other population of women; yet local services are lacking or do not exist in many tribal communities and Alaska Native villages. While states and territories receive an annual formula amount from the VOCA fund, the reality is that Indian tribes do not receive such an allocation and this must be remedied immediately. We urge an amendment to VOCA to direct 10 percent of the annual disbursement from the Crime Victims Fund to tribal governments. Thank you for this opportunity and for your leadership.

———

PREPARED STATEMENT OF HON. CARL JERUE, CHIEF, ANVIK TRIBAL COUNCIL

Dear Chairman Barrasso,

Thank you for the opportunity to provide written comments regarding the Oversight Hearing on "Addressing the Needs for Victim Services in Indian Country" held on June 10, 2015. The Village of Anvik respectfully requests that 42 U.S.C. 10602 (b) be amended to include, "Federally recognized Indian tribes" as eligible for the Victim Crimes Compensation fund. It is further our request that a minimum of 10 percent of authorized funds be Congressionally appropriated to American Indian and Alaska Native Tribal governments for the reasons described below.

A Change to VOCA is needed to Support Local Tribal Responses to High Crime Rates on Tribal Lands as Recommended by the Indian Law & Order Commission Report, "A Roadmap for Making Native America Safer"

American Indian and Alaska Natives experience the highest crime victimization rates in the country.

- American Indian and Alaska Natives are 2.5 times more likely to experience violent crime than other Americans.
- Approximately 34 percent of American Indian and Alaska Native women are raped and 61 percent are assaulted in their lifetime. One some reservations, the murder rate is 10 times the national average.
- Due to exposure to violence, Native children experience rates of post-traumatic stress disorder at the same levels as Iraq and Afghanistan war veterans.

Despite these devastating rates of victimization in tribal communities, Indian tribes have largely been left out of the Crime Victims Fund (CVF), which is the federal government's principle means of providing resources for crime victims.

It is beyond debate that Alaska Native women are suffering extreme rates of domestic violence and sexual assault—rates that are disproportionately higher than that suffered by other women in the state and across the nation. There is much work that needs to be done immediately to combat this crisis, to protect Alaska Native women from violence, to increase and strengthen local life-saving services and justice to Native women survivors of this violence. Providing essential accessible resources to Indian Tribes that reach the villages in Alaska will account for successful and fair administration of crime victim funding. It is also crucial for the equitable distribution of life-saving resources to Alaska tribal governments.

Unlike state and territorial governments, who receive an annual formula distribution from the CVF, Indian tribes are only able to access CVF funds via pass-through grants from the states or by competing for very limited resources administered by the U.S. Department of Justice. According to data from the Office for Victims of Crime, in 2014, the states passed through $872,197.00—0.2 percent of available funds—to programs serving tribal victims. Of the 566 federally recognized tribes in the country, fewer than 20 received pass through grants from their respective state.

The competitive grants from USDOJ have been equally problematic. Fewer than ten tribes receive these grants each year for a three-year term, with no guarantee that this funding will be renewed. Unfortunately, without additional action by Congress, Indian tribal governments will continue to have no direct access to critical CVF funds.

Appropriate Funding is needed to provide adequate Native Village-based Services

The villages in Alaska experience high victimization rates, geographic remoteness, high poverty and cost of living, and an underdeveloped Alaska Native village-based victim services infrastructure that is the result of the historic exclusion of tribes from the CVF programs. While we know need is high, it is difficult to calculate the precise amount needed to fully meet the needs of victims in Alaska Native villages. Below are some examples of funding needs for tribal victim services and how CVF funds could be spent.

Tribal Domestic Violence and Sexual Assault Services

Native American women are assaulted at rates two and a half times the national average. Alaska Native women are disproportionately victimized at the highest rates across the country. According to the Indian Law and Order Commission report, *A Roadmap for Making Native America Safe,* Chapter 2, *Reforming Justice for Alaska Natives: The Time Is Now,* Alaska Native women are "over-represented in the domestic violence victim population by 250 percent; they comprise 19 percent of the population, but 47 percent of reported rape victims."

While some tribes provide services for domestic violence and sexual assault victims, resources for doing so are woefully inadequate. NEED: For FY 2014, the USDOJ's Office on Violence Against Women received applications from tribal governments requesting approximately $55.6 million for domestic violence and sexual assault services in its two primary tribal grant programs. OVW provided $33.26 million, suggesting an unmet need of at least $22 million.

Tribal Domestic Violence Shelters

There are currently fewer than 40 tribal domestic violence shelters in operation. In the State of Alaska, there is only one Native village-based Native women's shelter located in the entire state—the Emmonak Women's Shelter, which has been operating since 1979 and has been woefully underfunded. More often than not, the Emmonak Women's Shelter has not received federal or state funding and remained operational with volunteer assistance and donations. Those programs that do exist reported an unmet need of over 60,000 shelter bed nights in 2013. NEED: Building a shelter program in an additional 50 villages and tribal communities at a cost of $300,000/year would cost $15 million.

Sexual Assault Forensic Examiners

The rate of sexual violence in Indian Country, including all of Alaska's tribes far exceeds rates of sexual violence in other communities in the United States. More than two-thirds of tribal lands, however, are more than 60 minutes away from the nearest sexual assault forensic examiner. With over 229 Indian tribes represented in Alaska, the vast majority of villages are located in the remote parts of Alaska where there are no roads; access is by boat, snow machine or airplane depending on climatic conditions. For Native women in Alaska, forensic exams typically are only located in hub regions, which means she must travel by plane to a major hub that may be over 200 air miles away. NEED: To fund one trained examiner in half of the 566 tribal communities at $50,000 for salary and benefits would cost $14 million.

Services for Sex Trafficking Victims

Sex trafficking victims need specially designed services, including victim advocates to connect sexually exploited youth throughout the state with culturally appropriate support and services they need; shelters and housing; and training for criminal justice and child protective services professionals who come into contact with such victims.

According to the State of Alaska Task Force on the *Crimes of Human Trafficking, Promoting Prostitution and Sex Trafficking* 2013 report, there is "a lot of gaps in information due to the underground nature of the crime and the tendency of trafficking victims not to self-report." Although lacking in data, the Task Force acknowledges that "trafficking have occurred (and likely are occurring) in Alaska, which is why the State of Alaska has gone to great lengths to create a task force to look at the prevalence of the crimes of human trafficking and sex trafficking in Alaska; the former Governor introduced an omnibus bill addressing trafficking (which strengthened penalties for trafficking); and in 2012 the Alaska legislature amended its sex and human trafficking statutes. NEED: To fund one trafficking advocate expert in half of the 566 tribal communities at $50,000 for salary and benefits would cost $14 million.

Services for the Survivors of Homicide Victims

Services for the surviving spouses, children, and other affected family members and partners of the victims of homicides are rarely funded but sorely needed. Between 2004–2007, Alaska Natives were 2.5 times as likely to die by homicide than Alaskans who reported "White" as their race, and 2.9 times as likely to die by homicide than all Whites in the United States.

Much needed services include criminal justice advocacy, assistance in applying for victim compensation, funding to travel to trials that are out of state, legal assistance, financial counseling if the murdered victim was the sole provider, mental health counseling or other therapy, and similar services. NEED: Iowa is the rare state that has committed to supporting regional services for survivors of homicide and other violent crimes. In FY 2014, the state used $393,441 in federal grant funds to support 4 regional programs for survivors of homicide and other violent crimes. Creating 25 such programs for tribal victims would cost approximately $2.5 million.

There is Wide Support for a Creation of a Tribal Funding Stream from the CVF

Last year, NCAI, the largest national organization of American Indian and Alaska Native tribal governments, adopted Resolution ANC–14–048 urging Congress to establish a 10 percent allocation from CVF disbursements for tribes.

Recognizing the disproportionate need for victim services in tribal communities, the Office for Victims of Crime's *Vision 21* report also called for increasing resources to tribal communities in order to "ensure that victims in Indian Country are no longer a footnote to this country's response to crime victims."

The USDOJ's report on American Indian and Alaska Native Children Exposed to Violence similarly called for a 10 percent tribal allocation from the CVF in its 2014 report. A 10 percent tribal allocation from the CVF has also been supported by the National Task Force to End Sexual and Domestic Violence, a coalition of more than a thousand organizations that advocate on behalf of victims of domestic violence, dating violence, sexual assault and stalking.

Conclusion

No dedicated tribal funding stream currently exists under the VOCA for Indian tribes to administer programs to compensate and provide assistance to tribal victims of crime. This lack of funding to Indian tribes is unacceptable given the extremely high rates of violence including the severity of violence committed against tribal victims of crime. The USDOJ statistics document the well-known fact that violence against Indian women is more than double that of any other population of women; yet local services are lacking or do not exist in many tribal communities and Alaska Native villages. While states and territories receive an annual formula amount from the VOCA fund, the reality is that Indian tribes do not receive such an allocation and this must be remedied immediately. We urge an amendment to VOCA to direct 10 percent of the annual disbursement from the Crime Victims Fund to tribal governments. Thank you for this opportunity and for your leadership.

PREPARED STATEMENT OF DARLENE M. PETE, TRIBAL ADMINISTRATOR, NATIVE VILLAGE OF NUNAM IQUA

Dear Chairman Barrasso,

Thank you for the opportunity to provide written comments regarding the Oversight Hearing on "Addressing the Needs for Victim Services in Indian Country" held on June 10, 2015. The Native Village of Nunam Iqua respectfully requests that 42

U.S.C. 10602 (b) be amended to include, ''Federally recognized Indian tribes'' as eligible for the Victim Crimes Compensation fund. It is further our request that a minimum of 10 percent of authorized funds be Congressionally appropriated to American Indian and Alaska Native Tribal governments for the reasons described below.

A Change to VOCA is needed to Support Local Tribal Responses to High Crime Rates on Tribal Lands as Recommended by the Indian Law & Order Commission Report, ''A Roadmap for Making Native America Safer''

American Indian and Alaska Natives experience the highest crime victimization rates in the country.

- American Indian and Alaska Natives are 2.5 times more likely to experience violent crime than other Americans.
- Approximately 34 percent of American Indian and Alaska Native women are raped and 61 percent are assaulted in their lifetime. One some reservations, the murder rate is 10 times the national average.
- Due to exposure to violence, Native children experience rates of post-traumatic stress disorder at the same levels as Iraq and Afghanistan war veterans.

Despite these devastating rates of victimization in tribal communities, Indian tribes have largely been left out of the Crime Victims Fund (CVF), which is the federal government's principle means of providing resources for crime victims.

It is beyond debate that Alaska Native women are suffering extreme rates of domestic violence and sexual assault—rates that are disproportionately higher than that suffered by other women in the state and across the nation. There is much work that needs to be done immediately to combat this crisis, to protect Alaska Native women from violence, to increase and strengthen local life-saving services and justice to Native women survivors of this violence. Providing essential accessible resources to Indian Tribes that reach the villages in Alaska will account for successful and fair administration of crime victim funding. It is also crucial for the equitable distribution of life-saving resources to Alaska tribal governments.

Unlike state and territorial governments, who receive an annual formula distribution from the CVF, Indian tribes are only able to access CVF funds via pass-through grants from the states or by competing for very limited resources administered by the U.S. Department of Justice. According to data from the Office for Victims of Crime, in 2014, the states passed through $872,197.00—0.2 percent of available funds—to programs serving tribal victims. Of the 566 federally recognized tribes in the country, fewer than 20 received pass through grants from their respective state.

The competitive grants from USDOJ have been equally problematic. Fewer than ten tribes receive these grants each year for a three-year term, with no guarantee that this funding will be renewed. Unfortunately, without additional action by Congress, Indian tribal governments will continue to have no direct access to critical CVF funds.

Appropriate Funding is needed to provide adequate Native Village-based Services

The villages in Alaska experience high victimization rates, geographic remoteness, high poverty and cost of living, and an underdeveloped Alaska Native village-based victim services infrastructure that is the result of the historic exclusion of tribes from the CVF programs. While we know need is high, it is difficult to calculate the precise amount needed to fully meet the needs of victims in Alaska Native villages. Below are some examples of funding needs for tribal victim services and how CVF funds could be spent.

Tribal Domestic Violence and Sexual Assault Services

Native American women are assaulted at rates two and a half times the national average. Alaska Native women are disproportionately victimized at the highest rates across the country. According to the Indian Law and Order Commission report, *A Roadmap for Making Native America Safe,* Chapter 2, *Reforming Justice for Alaska Natives: The Time Is Now,* Alaska Native women are ''over-represented in the domestic violence victim population by 250 percent; they comprise 19 percent of the population, but 47 percent of reported rape victims.''

While some tribes provide services for domestic violence and sexual assault victims, resources for doing so are woefully inadequate. NEED: For FY 2014, the USDOJ's Office on Violence Against Women received applications from tribal governments requesting approximately $55.6 million for domestic violence and sexual assault services in its two primary tribal grant programs. OVW provided $33.26 million, suggesting an unmet need of at least $22 million.

Tribal Domestic Violence Shelters

There are currently fewer than 40 tribal domestic violence shelters in operation. In the State of Alaska, there is only one Native village-based Native women's shelter located in the entire state—the Emmonak Women's Shelter, which has been operating since 1979 and has been woefully underfunded. More often than not, the Emmonak Women's Shelter has not received federal or state funding and remained operational with volunteer assistance and donations. Those programs that do exist reported an unmet need of over 60,000 shelter bed nights in 2013. NEED: Building a shelter program in an additional 50 villages and tribal communities at a cost of $300,000/year would cost $15 million.

Sexual Assault Forensic Examiners

The rate of sexual violence in Indian Country, including all of Alaska's tribes far exceeds rates of sexual violence in other communities in the United States. More than two-thirds of tribal lands, however, are more than 60 minutes away from the nearest sexual assault forensic examiner. With over 229 Indian tribes represented in Alaska, the vast majority of villages are located in the remote parts of Alaska where there are no roads; access is by boat, snow machine or airplane depending on climatic conditions. For Native women in Alaska, forensic exams typically are only located in hub regions, which means she must travel by plane to a major hub that may be over 200 air miles away. NEED: To fund one trained examiner in half of the 566 tribal communities at $50,000 for salary and benefits would cost $14 million.

Services for Sex Trafficking Victims

Sex trafficking victims need specially designed services, including victim advocates to connect sexually exploited youth throughout the state with culturally appropriate support and services they need; shelters and housing; and training for criminal justice and child protective services professionals who come into contact with such victims.

According to the State of Alaska Task Force on the *Crimes of Human Trafficking, Promoting Prostitution and Sex Trafficking* 2013 report, there is "a lot of gaps in information due to the underground nature of the crime and the tendency of trafficking victims not to self-report." Although lacking in data, the Task Force acknowledges that "trafficking have occurred (and likely are occurring) in Alaska, which is why the State of Alaska has gone to great lengths to create a task force to look at the prevalence of the crimes of human trafficking and sex trafficking in Alaska; the former Governor introduced an omnibus bill addressing trafficking (which strengthened penalties for trafficking); and in 2012 the Alaska legislature amended its sex and human trafficking statutes. NEED: To fund one trafficking advocate expert in half of the 566 tribal communities at $50,000 for salary and benefits would cost $14 million.

Services for the Survivors of Homicide Victims

Services for the surviving spouses, children, and other affected family members and partners of the victims of homicides are rarely funded but sorely needed. Between 2004–2007, Alaska Natives were 2.5 times as likely to die by homicide than Alaskans who reported "White" as their race, and 2.9 times as likely to die by homicide than all Whites in the United States.

Much needed services include criminal justice advocacy, assistance in applying for victim compensation, funding to travel to trials that are out of state, legal assistance, financial counseling if the murdered victim was the sole provider, mental health counseling or other therapy, and similar services. NEED: Iowa is the rare state that has committed to supporting regional services for survivors of homicide and other violent crimes. In FY 2014, the state used $393,441 in federal grant funds to support 4 regional programs for survivors of homicide and other violent crimes. Creating 25 such programs for tribal victims would cost approximately $2.5 million.

There is Wide Support for a Creation of a Tribal Funding Stream from the CVF

Last year, NCAI, the largest national organization of American Indian and Alaska Native tribal governments, adopted Resolution ANC–14–048 urging Congress to establish a 10 percent allocation from CVF disbursements for tribes.

Recognizing the disproportionate need for victim services in tribal communities, the Office for Victims of Crime's *Vision 21* report also called for increasing resources to tribal communities in order to "ensure that victims in Indian Country are no longer a footnote to this country's response to crime victims."

The USDOJ's report on American Indian and Alaska Native Children Exposed to Violence similarly called for a 10 percent tribal allocation from the CVF in its 2014 report. A 10 percent tribal allocation from the CVF has also been supported by the National Task Force to End Sexual and Domestic Violence, a coalition of more than a thousand organizations that advocate on behalf of victims of domestic violence, dating violence, sexual assault and stalking.

Conclusion

No dedicated tribal funding stream currently exists under the VOCA for Indian tribes to administer programs to compensate and provide assistance to tribal victims of crime. This lack of funding to Indian tribes is unacceptable given the extremely high rates of violence including the severity of violence committed against tribal victims of crime. The USDOJ statistics document the well-known fact that violence against Indian women is more than double that of any other population of women; yet local services are lacking or do not exist in many tribal communities and Alaska Native villages. While states and territories receive an annual formula amount from the VOCA fund, the reality is that Indian tribes do not receive such an allocation and this must be remedied immediately. We urge an amendment to VOCA to direct 10 percent of the annual disbursement from the Crime Victims Fund to tribal governments. Thank you for this opportunity and for your leadership.

PREPARED STATEMENT OF HON. MELVIN R. SHELDON, JR., CHAIRMAN, TULALIP TRIBES OF WASHINGTON

Dear Chairman Barrasso,

Thank you for the opportunity to provide written comments to the Oversight Hearing on Victim Services, held on June 10, 2015, "Addressing the Need for Victim Services in Indian Country." The Tulalip Tribes respectfully requests that the text in 42 U.S.C. 10602 (b) be amended to include, "Federally recognized Indian tribes" as eligible for Victim Crimes Compensation fund and that a *minimum* of 10% of authorized funds be Congressionally-appropriated to Tribal governmental programs for the following reasons set out below. American Indian and Alaska Natives experience the highest crime victimization rates in the country but are almost entirely left out of the programs funded through the Victims of Crime Act (VOCA).

Background on the Tulalip Tribes

The Tulalip Tribes are the successors in interest to the Snohomish, Snoqualmie, Skykomish, and other allied bands signatory to the 1855 Treaty of Point Elliott. The United States Constitution recognizes three distinct sovereigns in addition to the Federal government: the several states, foreign nations, and Indian Tribes. As a sovereign government, Tulalip Tribes' governing responsibilities mirror that of other sovereign governments. The Tulalip Tribes, as it has been for thousands of years, is a government exercising its powers to best determine the needs of its traditional territory and tribal citizens.

Decades of failed United States policy has resulted in a great need for many services in our tribal community. Tulalip culture, language, values, and spiritual beliefs were nearly eradicated under U.S. government superintendence. Furthermore, disruption of traditional ways of life has caused a variety of ills among our community, including a diabetes epidemic, chemical dependency problems, increased crime per capita and disproportionate poverty. The needs of the Tulalip Tribal community remain great. Our tribal government has developed many programs to provide benefits to our citizens to respond to these problems, but there is still a great need for financial assistance.

Why a change in VOCA funding is needed

Tribally-based victim services program need to have direct access to victim funds equal to victims in state and federal systems. Sustained, adequate funding to create highest-quality services for the most vulnerable and most heavily victimized population in the nation is critical. Permanent tribal set-aside funding for crime victims is imperative if tribal victims are to receive adequate, quality, trauma-informed care. The funding that is currently available to tribes is highly competitive, relatively meager as compared to the need, time-limited, and often carries with it restrictions that hobble innovation, stability and excellence in tribal victim services.

Both the domestic violence program and the children's advocacy program at Tulalip Tribes share a horrifying statistic: 100% of the victims we see suffer from poly-victimization. What this means has become clear through research by those such as David Finkelhor, Ph.D. Director of the Crimes Against Children Research Center and Co-Director of the Family Research Laboratory, who has extensively researched the issue. Children who suffer from poly-victimization should be prioritized for quality services:

"Professionals who work with children need to pay particular attention to polyvictims because of their vulnerability to mental health, behavioral, school performance, and other problems. These children can be identified in schools, in social welfare and mental health caseloads, and in the foster care and juvenile justice systems; and they warrant priority in victimization interventions."[1]

It is also well understood that there are disproportionately high rates of victimization and incarceration of juvenile tribal youth, with low or no direct funding to tribally-based direct services and interventions.

The 2012, the National Task Force on Children Exposed to Violence determined that:
- AI/AN [American Indian/Alaska Native] children have a significant degree of unmet needs for services and support to prevent and respond to the extreme levels of violence they experience;
- The federal government has a unique legal responsibility for the welfare of AI/AN children;
- The federal government also has a special relationship with Indian tribes based, at least in part, on its trust responsibility; and
- AI/AN communities confront additional burdens in meeting the needs of children exposed to violence.

Cultural competency in specialized forensic interviewers and victim advocates is paramount to providing meaningful services to tribal victims, and to engaging victims and their families in services post-trauma. The challenge that we face in striving for a safer community for children is well described by Paul Steele, Director of the Center for Justice Studies at Morehead State University:

Children living on the cultural margins of society are more likely to experience negative life outcomes for two reasons: First, their disempowered position exposes them to greater social risks and limits their ability to

---

[1] Finkelhor, D., Turner, H.A., Hamby, S.L. and Ormrod, R.K.(2011). Poly-victimization: Children's Exposure of Multiple Types of Violence, Crime and Abuse. OJJDP Juvenile Justice Bulletin – NCJ235504 (pgs. 1-12). Washington, DC: US Government Printing Office.

protect themselves. Second, agencies and institutions intended to protect children from harm are less effective in resolving cases in which they are involved, compared to children from more privileged backgrounds.[2]

In developing the Tulalip victim services' program, it was quickly apparent that state and county systems were not meeting the needs of children "living on the cultural margins" in the Tulalip community. In addition, Child Protection Services and Indian Child Welfare struggled to keep stable, well-trained social workers. Because of the chronically high turnover and inadequate training in complex cases, grossly over-burdened F.B.I. Agents and Victim Specialists covered far too much territory, and prosecutors often had few or no ties to the community and at times showed little zeal and regard for tribal community safety. Over the years, many of these barriers have been removed when highly qualified, passionate professionals have remained at the tribe, becoming true team members in the fight to serve children. Some of these barriers remain a constant, such as the F.B.I.'s gross understaffing of Agents and Victim Specialists in Indian Country. While we have had many cases prosecuted in Federal court in recent years, we have not found the Federal Court Victim-Witness program to have any measurable impact on victims and families here on the reservation and may have been focusing their attention outside of the country! When staff attended a training, years ago, a high level staff member from our local Federal District Court Victim-Witness program presented at an event and highlighted work she was doing in Thailand to assist the government there in developing a victim's services program. Why isn't such staff focusing on domestic needs right here in this service area. To this day we have not received any meaningful service from that program.

History of the Tulalip Child Advocacy Center and impacts of Tribal-based CACs.

In 2007, the Tulalip Tribes dedicated resources to build a program to serve child sexual abuse victims, using the holistic Child Advocacy Center (CAC) model. There is a CAC in our neighboring city of Everett, Washington. This raised the question of why the Tribes would need their own CAC, when the mainstream CAC ostensibly served our community. Indian Child Welfare leaders and the detectives investigating violent crimes insisted that we needed a tribal-based CAC. At the outset, the Tribal CAC attempted to partner with the mainstream CAC, but it quickly became clear why we needed our own. Attempts to initiate discussions about leveraging resources and partnering to provide services to tribal children who were victims of sexual violence were met with comments that we should bring our victims directly to them, since they were the experts. However, that program was so enmeshed with internal politics that it became clear we would be last in line to schedule child forensic interviews. Furthermore, their restrictive protocol also meant that some children never received interviews. In addition, we experienced first-hand the dangers of using child interviewers with little cultural training, and its direct impacts on child interviews. Using their systems, we saw many times, children shutting down early in an interview when they realized the interviewer did not understand certain vernacular, cultural terms, or references to cultural practices. When it came time to disclose the most violent episodes of their lives, they clearly had decided that the interviewer was not going to understand them.

A child's testimony is always critical in every child abuse investigation and prosecution. Every time a case is not investigated in a timely manner due to inadequate resources, including lack of interviewers, advocates or investigators, the likelihood of a denial or limited disclosure rises. When violence abounds in a community, and there is little accountability from the systems designed to protect the community, trauma continues. In this way, a healthy, vital, healing community will never be possible.

---

[2] Steele, P.D., "Child Abuse Among Marginalized Groups: Cultural and Governmental Influences on the Perpetuation of Sexual Maltreatment in American Indian Country." FORUM ON PUBLIC POLICY, Vol. 5, No. 1, 2009: 1-33.

Sustainability needs of a Tribal CAC

Our program grew initially through an OVC Tribal Victim Assistance grant award, which allowed us to partially fund a coordinator to facilitate an MDT, and to train and hire a child forensic interviewer. A second grant allowed us to fund a child advocate. The Tribes allowed us to bring over a child therapist from another agency to create a comprehensive program, using tribal money. Since then, the Tribes have gradually taken on more financial responsibility for the program costs, including now fully funding the child advocate and the child therapist, and providing the CAC with a large building and costs of renovation to expand and improve our services. In spite of successfully competing for OVC funding for victims, we have never received funding adequate to cover our comprehensive program's costs. The cost of staffing our program on an annual basis exceeds $300,000 with minimal staffing. In 2014 the Tribes directly funded $214,000 of our costs, while grants funded $86,000.

Competent staff is mandatory

To address the needs of child victims, or any victims of violence, hiring and keeping highly competent staff is absolutely crucial. Gaining trust in the community is invaluable to navigate the complexities of working in a small, relatively insular community, and trust cannot be sustained absent high levels of competency. Our staff consists of a Coordinator/Director, a child forensic interviewer/child therapist, a full-time child therapist, a child advocate and a part-time office assistant. The Director/Coordinator endeavors to facilitate a high-functioning Multi-Disciplinary Team addressing child abuse, supervises and trains staff and other allied professionals, and guides child abuse cases despite constant turnover of investigators, prosecutors and CPS workers. Fundraising through grant writing and grant management has been the job of the Coordinator, as well. To find and keep culturally competent, highly qualified trauma-trained child therapists and advocates who are equipped to face daily trauma exposure is not an easy, nor an inexpensive effort.

Pass-through (State) funding is not appropriate

While fundraising has always been necessary and the highest priority as we have developed the Child Advocacy Center, we have never received funds from the State of Washington, VOCA funds. We found that while there are funds for "marginalized communities," for which we would qualify to compete, the grant amounts are small, the length of funding is short, and include onerous reporting requirements. In addition, the prescriptive qualities of the grants have always made competing for this funding source non-viable.

Tribes need flexibility in defining spending

The federal grants available through OVC have become, over the years, more and more prescriptive as well. Cooperative Agreements have replaced outright grants and some, such as Children's Justice Act funding, are so restrictive in spending limits that expenditures are not always on tribally-defined priorities. Tribal programs need high quality and more staff to do the work. The work of weaving together various funding streams, related administration, and constantly re-applying for short term funding is no way to make real progress in healing a community. While it is recognized that collaboration is the key to meeting the needs of victims, some funder decisions, such as the Office of Violence Against Women's requirement to spend money only on domestic violence direct service programming, and the Office of Victims of Crime forbidding expenditures on anything smacking of "prevention" simply forces the rebuilding of silos, and hobbles creativity and responsiveness to a community's unique needs.

The intersect of women and children's needs

The Tulalip Tribes has had a Domestic Violence program since 2000. At first, the program was placed in the Indian child welfare department and started out with one advocate. Over the years we have successfully applied for available grants to add needed components to grow the program and provide more comprehensive services for our community. However, just as the CAC saw that the more services provided, the more trusting the community becomes with these services, and the greater the need. Many victims, whose voices went unheard previously are now trusting the system and taking a chance that the crimes and other incidents committed against them, will be addressed. As previously mentioned these are some of the most vulnerable people of our communities, who because historical and intergenerational trauma, have multiple needs. Almost all of the women that we serve have children who are either direct victims or are present in the home during the domestic violence.

According to a Native American "Adverse Childhood Exposure" (ACE) original study, "...16% of the participants had 4 or more ACE's – One source has estimated the percentage of American Indians with 4 or more ACE's at 33% or double that of the total population."[1] Along with the fact that Native American women experience the highest levels of sexual and domestic abuse of any group, and according to the American Indian Women's Chemical Health Project, 3/4 of them have experienced some type of sexual assault in their lives. However, these statistics do not account for the 70 % of victims that do not report.

Since we opened the Legacy of Healing's Safe House in 2014, 100% of the women that were screened in and became residents at the Safe House reported experiencing multi-abuse trauma. We have found that the majority of our residents have been disconnected from their tribal communities, because they are not only surviving domestic and/or sexual violence, they're surviving multiple domestic violence relationships and sexual assaults. They have often grown up in, or lived in homes, where their traditional ways have been replaced with violence and substance abuse. They have become the most vulnerable victims resulting in homelessness, single parenting or even losing custody of their children, substance abuse, in or out of recovery, severe untreated or treated mental health issues such as: Post Traumatic Stress Disorder; Eating Disorders; Fetal Alcohol Syndrome or Effects; Self-Harm and Suicidal Tendencies. We have found also that because of these multiple issues, about 50% are unable to follow through with their Service Plans, which results in their ineligibility for other housing programs, and related services.

Without stable systems in place, that can account for these multiple needs it may be just a matter of time before these women go back to their abusers, find another abuser; taken advantage of by their abusers or family members, lose custody of their children, and end up on the streets, beaten and back in the hospital or dead. People often label this population of women as "throw-a-ways." In hindsight, we knew that we would be serving a population of women often with long-term victimization issues; however, we were not prepared for the magnitude of services needed in order to work with this very vulnerable population.

[1] Koss et al., Adverse Childhood Exposure and Alcohol Dependence Among Seven Native American Tribes, AM J Prev Med 2003; 25 (3): 238-244.

The crisis of children witnessing violence is even more critical in our Native American homes and communities. "Rates of crime and violence in some tribal areas are alarmingly high, often exceeding and sometimes dwarfing those of other jurisdictions, leading to the reasonable conclusion that native children are at especially high risk. As one tribal leader stated that for those in Indian country "…the question is not who has been exposed to violence, it's who hasn't been exposed to violence."

The victimization of Tulalip's children is one of the Tribes principal concerns and the Tribe has taken an active effort in protecting their youth from perpetrators; however, the tribe has not been able to adequately address the negative effects of children who have been exposed to sexual assault, domestic violence, family violence, dating violence, and stalking within their home. Women Advocates and Indian Child Welfare experts are increasingly aware of the effects of violence on children in the household and have often observed these same children coming of age and being re-victimized and/or perpetrators of violence; thus the cycle of violence continues.

VAWA 2013: Case Statistics of a Pilot Project

The Tulalip Tribes in its first year of exercising Special Domestic Violence Jurisdiction as a pilot project tribe, charged 7 individuals. Of these individuals, 3 have been convicted or plead guilty, 1 case was transferred for federal prosecution because of the severity of charges and will be jointly prosecuted between our DV Prosecutor/SAUSA and the AUSA, 1 case was dismissed for insufficient facts and 2 are awaiting trial. Children were present in 5 cases and in 2 of the cases children were assaulted. Of these 2 cases, only 1 defendant will be charged because it is in federal court and the other case will go uncharged for lack of tribal jurisdiction and lack of interest by the state. In 2 of the cases, the female victim was sexually assaulted. Of the 7 defendants, 6 of them were in current meretricious relationships with the victim and lived in the home. The tribal police had 90 civil and criminal prior contacts with these 7 defendants. While this jurisdiction is barely past its first year, the impact to victims of those perpetrators is great. While we have programs to provide some services, only the victim in the federal court, will be eligible for comprehensive VOCA victim services for her and her child as VOCA direct victim services are not provided to tribal court victims.

Summary of Key Points to Consider

- Infrastructure needs: As more victims trust the criminal and judicial systems, more victims emerge and the existing programs need to expand as well as be sustained to meet the need. Our programs are still crisis-based; our communities still need to heal. There is significant need.
- Competitive Funding v. Sustainability Plans: We respectfully request that OVW and VOCA funding move away from competitive funding and provide block grants to tribes. We need on-going funding that our programs can depend upon. Any formula considered should be based on a tribal-consulted formula based on current levels and program needs, and not on revised state formulas.
- We need more money for program development. We have been part of surveys and studies of population served. Our clients have long standing victimization, and oftentimes from previous generations. These women and children need complete and comprehensive services. Many were abused as children, then as women, thus they have chronic substance abuse and mental health issues. Many have children, may be homeless and actively using alcohol and/or drugs. We need funding for "therapeutic housing." We need a wrap-around team in our shelters that include detoxification, CD counselors, MH counselors, life skills counselors and other related support.

- We need funding for training in a manner that is consistent with the tribe, which means being able to provide food. It is our culture to provide food to our guests. In addition we need funding sources for training related costs such as overtime for police officers and other staff to attend training.
- We need funding levels to increase so that we can attract and retain the best people for the job. We are fortunate that Tulalip has funded through hard dollars many staff and programs. However, each year we have to fight for those sustained dollars as tribal needs across the spectrum are great.

Conclusion

In summary, while OVW has made great strides in funding programs to serve adult victims of violence a lot of work and funding is still needed. Children do, and always will, depend on adults to carry their voice. We implore Congress to act and amend VOCA to include Tribal Governments to directly access VOCA funds with a minimum of a Congressionally-appropriated 10% annual disbursement. Please direct any questions or further requests for input related to children to Leila Goldsmith at lgoldsmith@tulaliptribes-nsn.gov and for input related to adult victim programs, to Roxanne Chinook at rchinook@tulaliptribes-nsn.gov. t'igwicid, or thank you for this opportunity to provide information to the Senate Select Committee on Indian Affairs.

PREPARED STATEMENT OF HON. IVAN M. IVAN, CHIEF, AKIAK NATIVE COMMUNITY

Dear Chairman Barrasso,

Thank you for the opportunity to provide written comments regarding the Oversight Hearing on "Addressing the Needs for Victim Services in Indian Country" held on June 10, 2015. The Akiak IRA Council respectfully requests that 42 U.S.C. 10602 (b) be amended to include, "Federally recognized Indian tribes" as eligible for the Victim Crimes Compensation fund. It is further our request that a minimum of 10 percent of authorized funds be Congressionally appropriated to American Indian and Alaska Native Tribal governments for the reasons described below.

A Change to VOCA is needed to Support Local Tribal Responses to High Crime Rates on Tribal Lands as Recommended by the Indian Law & Order Commission Report, "A Roadmap for Making Native America Safer"

American Indian and Alaska Natives experience the highest crime victimization rates in the country.

- American Indian and Alaska Natives are 2.5 times more likely to experience violent crime than other Americans.
- Approximately 34 percent of American Indian and Alaska Native women are raped and 61 percent are assaulted in their lifetime. One some reservations, the murder rate is 10 times the national average.
- Due to exposure to violence, Native children experience rates of post-traumatic stress disorder at the same levels as Iraq and Afghanistan war veterans.

Despite these devastating rates of victimization in tribal communities, Indian tribes have largely been left out of the Crime Victims Fund (CVF), which is the federal government's principle means of providing resources for crime victims.

It is beyond debate that Alaska Native women are suffering extreme rates of domestic violence and sexual assault—rates that are disproportionately higher than that suffered by other women in the state and across the nation. There is much work that needs to be done immediately to combat this crisis, to protect Alaska Native women from violence, to increase and strengthen local life-saving services and justice to Native women survivors of this violence. Providing essential accessible resources to Indian Tribes that reach the villages in Alaska will account for successful and fair administration of crime victim funding. It is also crucial for the equitable distribution of life-saving resources to Alaska tribal governments.

Unlike state and territorial governments, who receive an annual formula distribution from the CVF, Indian tribes are only able to access CVF funds via pass-through grants from the states or by competing for very limited resources administered by the U.S. Department of Justice. According to data from the Office for Victims of Crime, in 2014, the states passed through $872,197.00—0.2 percent of available funds—to programs serving tribal victims. Of the 566 federally recognized tribes in the country, fewer than 20 received pass through grants from their respective state.

The competitive grants from USDOJ have been equally problematic. Fewer than ten tribes receive these grants each year for a three-year term, with no guarantee that this funding will be renewed. Unfortunately, without additional action by Congress, Indian tribal governments will continue to have no direct access to critical CVF funds.

Appropriate Funding is needed to provide adequate Native Village-based Services

The villages in Alaska experience high victimization rates, geographic remoteness, high poverty and cost of living, and an underdeveloped Alaska Native village-based victim services infrastructure that is the result of the historic exclusion of tribes from the CVF programs. While we know need is high, it is difficult to calculate the precise amount needed to fully meet the needs of victims in Alaska Native villages. Below are some examples of funding needs for tribal victim services and how CVF funds could be spent.

Tribal Domestic Violence and Sexual Assault Services

Native American women are assaulted at rates two and a half times the national average. Alaska Native women are disproportionately victimized at the highest rates across the country. According to the Indian Law and Order Commission report, *A Roadmap for Making Native America Safe,* Chapter 2, *Reforming Justice for Alaska Natives: The Time Is Now,* Alaska Native women are "over-represented in the domestic violence victim population by 250 percent; they comprise 19 percent of the population, but 47 percent of reported rape victims."

While some tribes provide services for domestic violence and sexual assault victims, resources for doing so are woefully inadequate. NEED: For FY 2014, the USDOJ's Office on Violence Against Women received applications from tribal governments requesting approximately $55.6 million for domestic violence and sexual assault services in its two primary tribal grant programs. OVW provided $33.26 million, suggesting an unmet need of at least $22 million.

Tribal Domestic Violence Shelters

There are currently fewer than 40 tribal domestic violence shelters in operation. In the State of Alaska, there is only one Native village-based Native women's shelter located in the entire state—the Emmonak Women's Shelter, which has been operating since 1979 and has been woefully underfunded. More often than not, the Emmonak Women's Shelter has not received federal or state funding and remained operational with volunteer assistance and donations. Those programs that do exist reported an unmet need of over 60,000 shelter bed nights in 2013. NEED: Building a shelter program in an additional 50 villages and tribal communities at a cost of $300,000/year would cost $15 million.

Sexual Assault Forensic Examiners

The rate of sexual violence in Indian Country, including all of Alaska's tribes far exceeds rates of sexual violence in other communities in the United States. More than two-thirds of tribal lands, however, are more than 60 minutes away from the nearest sexual assault forensic examiner. With over 229 Indian tribes represented in Alaska, the vast majority of villages are located in the remote parts of Alaska where there are no roads; access is by boat, snow machine or airplane depending on climatic conditions. For Native women in Alaska, forensic exams typically are only located in hub regions, which means she must travel by plane to a major hub that may be over 200 air miles away. NEED: To fund one trained examiner in half of the 566 tribal communities at $50,000 for salary and benefits would cost $14 million.

Services for Sex Trafficking Victims

Sex trafficking victims need specially designed services, including victim advocates to connect sexually exploited youth throughout the state with culturally appropriate support and services they need; shelters and housing; and training for criminal justice and child protective services professionals who come into contact with such victims.

According to the State of Alaska Task Force on the *Crimes of Human Trafficking, Promoting Prostitution and Sex Trafficking* 2013 report, there is "a lot of gaps in information due to the underground nature of the crime and the tendency of trafficking victims not to self-report." Although lacking in data, the Task Force acknowledges that "trafficking have occurred (and likely are occurring) in Alaska, which is why the State of Alaska has gone to great lengths to create a task force to look at the prevalence of the crimes of human trafficking and sex trafficking in Alaska; the former Governor introduced an omnibus bill addressing trafficking (which strengthened penalties for trafficking); and in 2012 the Alaska legislature amended its sex and human trafficking statutes. NEED: To fund one trafficking advocate expert in half of the 566 tribal communities at $50,000 for salary and benefits would cost $14 million.

Services for the Survivors of Homicide Victims

Services for the surviving spouses, children, and other affected family members and partners of the victims of homicides are rarely funded but sorely needed. Between 2004–2007, Alaska Natives were 2.5 times as likely to die by homicide than Alaskans who reported "White" as their race, and 2.9 times as likely to die by homicide than all Whites in the United States.

Much needed services include criminal justice advocacy, assistance in applying for victim compensation, funding to travel to trials that are out of state, legal assistance, financial counseling if the murdered victim was the sole provider, mental health counseling or other therapy, and similar services. NEED: Iowa is the rare state that has committed to supporting regional services for survivors of homicide and other violent crimes. In FY 2014, the state used $393,441 in federal grant funds to support 4 regional programs for survivors of homicide and other violent crimes. Creating 25 such programs for tribal victims would cost approximately $2.5 million.

There is Wide Support for a Creation of a Tribal Funding Stream from the CVF

Last year, NCAI, the largest national organization of American Indian and Alaska Native tribal governments, adopted Resolution ANC–14–048 urging Congress to establish a 10 percent allocation from CVF disbursements for tribes.

Recognizing the disproportionate need for victim services in tribal communities, the Office for Victims of Crime's *Vision 21* report also called for increasing resources to tribal communities in order to ''ensure that victims in Indian Country are no longer a footnote to this country's response to crime victims.''

The USDOJ's report on American Indian and Alaska Native Children Exposed to Violence similarly called for a 10 percent tribal allocation from the CVF in its 2014 report. A 10 percent tribal allocation from the CVF has also been supported by the National Task Force to End Sexual and Domestic Violence, a coalition of more than a thousand organizations that advocate on behalf of victims of domestic violence, dating violence, sexual assault and stalking.

Conclusion

No dedicated tribal funding stream currently exists under the VOCA for Indian tribes to administer programs to compensate and provide assistance to tribal victims of crime. This lack of funding to Indian tribes is unacceptable given the extremely high rates of violence including the severity of violence committed against tribal victims of crime. The USDOJ statistics document the well-known fact that violence against Indian women is more than double that of any other population of women; yet local services are lacking or do not exist in many tribal communities and Alaska Native villages. While states and territories receive an annual formula amount from the VOCA fund, the reality is that Indian tribes do not receive such an allocation and this must be remedied immediately. We urge an amendment to VOCA to direct 10 percent of the annual disbursement from the Crime Victims Fund to tribal governments. Thank you for this opportunity and for your leadership.

———

JOINT PREPARED STATEMENT OF RUTH FLOWER AND HANNAH EVANS, FRIENDS COMMITTEE ON NATIONAL LEGISLATION

Dear Senators:

As advocates for our respective faith traditions and the values they uphold, one area of particular concern for us is our nation's relationship with Native Americans and their tribal governments. We write to you today to address two concerns about the release of funds collected through the Crime Victims Fund.

As you know, the Crime Victims Fund (CVF) provides critical funding to states for services for survivors of sexual and domestic violence. Collections for this fund, which come from perpetrators of violent crimes, have accumulated impressively. According to the Department of Justice, this fund had a balance of more than $13 billion in FY 2013. While nearly $2.8 billion was collected in 2013, the fund only released about $700 million each year for the past several years. For FY 2015, Congress released $2.36 billion, for which we are deeply grateful.

Our concern is that the CVF is not being utilized to its fullest potential. Many victims do not receive the services they need because Congress has not mandated that the Fund disperse what it collects on an annual basis. A more substantial, stable source of support would enable local service agencies to help more victims make their lives whole again.

A second concern is in regard to access to these funds by Native American tribal governments. Native American women are particularly vulnerable to violence, with violent crimes occurring on reservations at about 2.5 times the national average, and murders of Native women at 10 times the national average on some reservations. Yet tribal governments do not have direct access to the Crime Victims Fund as other governments do. Tribal governments must ask states to share their allocation from the Crime Victims Fund, or apply for a federal grant. Tribal governments need a consistent and reliable source of funds for programs that serve victims of violence on their reservation, and perhaps even more importantly, for programs that prevent and address the root causes of violence.

Violence has a particularly devastating impact on youth. Since Native Americans are victimized by crime at disproportionately high rates, each generation of Native youth is permanently injured by violence, whether they are victim themselves, or they see the effects of violence in their families and in their community. The funds provided through Crime Victims Fund and related federal grant programs can help to interrupt this cycle and, as much as possible, make victims whole.

To address these two problems, we urge you to enact legislation that would require the Department of Justice to annually disperse from the Crime Victims Fund an amount equal to the average of the past three years' deposits, so that all victims of crime can adequately access the support they deserve.

Secondly we ask that Congress create a dedicated funding stream from the Crime Victims Fund for tribal governments so that this particularly impacted community has direct access to funding to provide continuity of care to victims of crime. Finally, we ask that if legislation is not passed to resolve these issues, appropriators set aside adequate and dedicated funding from the Crime Victims Fund for tribal governments.

Congress can act to ensure than no rape crisis center needs to have a waiting list, no safe house needs to turn away a victim—leaving her vulnerable to her abuser. No counseling, support, and prevention center would need to minimize these important types of assistance, in favor of emergency interventions to stop the beatings. As people of faith committed to ensuring all victims of crime receive adequate, consistent, and reliable support, we urge you to enact these simple and just policy recommendations.

> AMERICAN FRIENDS SERVICE COMMITTEE
> FRANCISCAN ACTION NETWORK
> JESUIT CONFERENCE OF CANADA AND THE UNITED STATES
> NETWORK: A NATIONAL CATHOLIC SOCIAL JUSTICE LOBBY
> OFFICE OF SOCIAL JUSTICE OF THE CHRISTIAN REFORMED
> CHURCH PAX CHRISTI USA
> PRESBYTERIAN CHURCH (U.S.A.)
> SISTERS OF MERCY OF THE AMERICAS—INSTITUTE JUSTICE TEAM
> UNION FOR REFORM JUDAISM
> UNITED CHURCH OF CHRIST, JUSTICE AND WITNESS MINISTRIES
> UNITED METHODIST CHURCH-GENERAL BOARD OF CHURCH AND SOCIETY
> FRIENDS COMMITTEE ON NATIONAL LEGISLATION

LETTER SUBMITTED BY JERRY GARDNER, EXECUTIVE DIRECTOR, TRIBAL LAW AND POLICY INSTITUTE

Honorable John Culberson, Chairman
U.S. House of Representatives

Honorable Chaka Fattah, Ranking Member
House Appropriations Committee

Subcommittee on Commerce, Justice, Science & Related Agencies,
Washington, D.C.

RE: AVAILABILITY OF CRIME VICTIMS FUND FOR TRIBAL GOVERNMENTS

Dear Chairman Culberson and Ranking Member Fattah,

On behalf of the Tribal Law and Policy Institute (TLPI) , a Native American owned and operated non-profit organized to promote the enhancement of justice in Indian country and the health, well-being, and culture of Native peoples. I am writing to ask for your help in addressing a long-standing inequity that leaves American Indian/Alaska Native victims of crime without access to the assistance and compensation that others receive. Specifically, we are requesting that Indian tribes be included as direct recipients of the annual distributions from the Crime Victims Fund(CVF).

American Indian and Alaska Natives are 2.5 times more likely to experience violent crime than other Americans. Due to exposure to violence, Native children experience rates of post-traumatic stress disorder at the same levels as Iraq and Afghanistan war veterans. However, only a tiny fraction of CVF monies, the federal government's principle means of providing resources for crime victims, are made directly available to tribes.

Currently, state and territorial governments receive an annual formal distribution from the CVF. Tribes are eligible to apply to a state for funding, but only 0.2 percent of available of funds ($872,197) were actually distributed in 2014. Ofthe 566 federally recognized tribes in the country, fewer than 20 received a pass-through grant from a state.

The competitive grants from the Department of Justice (DOJ) have been equally problematic. Fewer than ten tribes receive these grants each year for a three-year term, with no guarantee that funding will be renewed. Often when a grant ends, tribal programs must completely shut down. Given that much of Indian Country is geographically isolated, if tribal programs are not available, then victims have no access to help.

Last year, the National Congress of American Indians (NCAI) adopted Resolution ANC–14–048 urging Congress to establish a 10 percent allocation from CVF disbursements for tribal governments.

> **NOW THEREFORE BE IT RESOLVED,** that the NCAI does hereby support the increase in the amount of money released from the Crime Victim's Fund to include a dedicated funding stream for Indian tribes to meet the dire needs of tribal victims; and
>
> **BE IT FURTHER RESOLVED,** that the NCAI does hereby support the creation of an "above the cap" reserve in the Victims of Crime Act (VOCA), or alternatively, a 10 percent VOCA tribal set-aside, that would fund tribes and tribal government programs and non-profit, non-governmental tribal organizations, located within the jurisdictional boundaries of an Indian reservation, Alaska Native Villages, and Indian areas that provide services to Native women victimized by domestic and/or sexual violence.[1]

Recognizing the disproportionate need for victim services in tribal communities, the Office for Victims of Crime's *Vision 21* report also called for increasing resources to tribal communities in order to "ensure that victims in Indian Country are no longer a footnote to this country's response to crime victims." The Attorney General's Task Force on American Indian and Alaska Native Children Exposed to Violence similarly called for a 10 percent tribal allocation from the CVF in its 2014 report.

> Recommendation 1.4.E Congress shall establish a much larger commitment than currently exists to fund tribal programs through the Department of Justice's Office of Justice Programs (OJP) and the Victims of Crime Act (VOCA) funding. As an initial step towards the much larger commitment needed, Congress shall establish a minimum 10 percent tribal set-aside, as per the Violence Against Women Act (VAWA) tribal set-aside, from funding for all discretionary Office of Justice Program (OJP) and Victims of Crime Act (VOCA) funding making clear that the tribal set-aside is the minimum tribal funding and not in any way a cap on tribal funding. President Obama's annual budget request to Congress has included a 7 percent tribal set-aside for the last few years. This is a very positive step and Congress should authorize this request immediately. However, the set-aside should be increased to 10 percent in subsequent appropriation bills. Until Congress act, the Department of Justice (DOJ) shall establish this minimum 10 percent tribal set-aside administratively.[2]

A 10 percent tribal allocation has also been supported by the National Task Force to End Sexual and Domestic Violence, a coalition of more than a thousand organizations that advocate on behalf of victims of domestic violence, dating violence, sexual assault and stalking

In recent years, annual distributions from the CVF have been about $700 million. Collections, however, reached as high as $2.8 billion in 2013, leaving a balance in the fund of more than $12 billion. There has been significant pressure on Congress to make this money available for crime victims, and Congress significantly increased the distributions for FY 2015 to $2.3 billion. Despite this three-fold increase, none of the money was directed to Indian tribes. There is language in the FY 2016 Budget Resolution that would remove any incentive for appropriators to return to the lower level of disbursement, and we expect that disbursements from the CVF this year may well exceed $2.5 billion. With this significant increase in funding, now is the time to make sure that crime victims in tribal communities are no longer shut out of the crime victim assistance and compensation that they desperately need.

---

[1] National Congress of American Indians Resolution #ANC–14–048, "Support for a dedicated Tribal Set-Aside in the Victims of Crime Act (VOCA) Fund," (June 11, 2014), *available at http://www.ncai.org/attachments/Resolu-tion*lsetxfZPHiQTTzySUNFbXPGMQbWeImEpTlwnDJOrYdpnOLIJlyiUlANC–14–048.pdf

[2] ATTORNEY GENERAL'S ADVISORY COMMITTEE ON AMERICAN INDIAN AND ALASKA NATIVE CHILDREN EXPOSED TO VIOLENCE, U.S. DEP'T OF JUSTICE, REPORT OF THE ADVISORY COMMITTEE ON AMERICAN INDIAN AND ALASKA NATIVE CHILDREN EXPOSED TO VIOLENCE: ENDING VIOLENCE SO CHILDREN CAN THRIVE 59, Recommendation 1.4.E (November 2014) [hereinafter ENDING VIOLENCE SO CHILDREN CAN THRIVE REPORT], full final report found at: *http://www.justice.gov/sites/default/files/defendingchildhood/pages/attachments/2015/03/23/end-ing*lviolencelsolchildrenlcanlthrive.pdf

We urge you to include language in the CJS appropriations bill that will direct a portion of the disbursements from the Crime Victims Fund to tribal governments. We greatly appreciate your leadership on this issue.